THE ACADEMIC HUSTLE

Praise for *The Academic Hustle*

"*An insightful guide for students and parents! The author is a product of Morehouse College which instills in graduates a strong ethic of 'lifting others as we climb'.* The Academic Hustle *is filled with nuggets of insight and wit from one who succeeded against the odds and aims to inspire others to academic achievement and personal fulfillment.*"

—Dr. Robert M. Franklin, President Emeritus of Morehouse College

"*The 100 Black Men of America, Inc. has mentored thousands of youth to career achievement. Matthew is one of our best. Through* The Academic Hustle, *he distills the wisdom gained from his national award-winning research on our members and his personal transformation into a manual for excellence in education and beyond.*"

—Al Dotson, Chairman Emeritus, 100 Black Men of America, Inc.

"*As a college president, this is the book I have been waiting for! Matthew's personal transformation, combined with a clear game plan for how students can finance their college education, strikes the perfect balance between inspiration and action.*"

—Dr. Roslyn Clark Artis, President of Benedict College

"If parents and students follow this game plan, they will not have to worry about money for school or what to do after graduation. The Academic Hustle *truly is the ultimate game plan for academic achievement."*

—Mr. David Watkins, Director of Equity and Academic Attainment for Broward Public Schools

"How to pay for college is the number one obstacle that prohibits too many students with great potential from earning a degree. This guide offers insightful and innovative ideas about how to achieve that goal without amassing massive debt, which will enable young people to focus on what's most important—building bright futures."

—Congresswoman Frederica S. Wilson (D-24 Florida)

THE ACADEMIC HUSTLE:

The Ultimate Game Plan for Scholarships, Internships, and Job Offers

Matthew A. Pigatt

Mango Publishing
Coral Gables

Cover & Layout Design: Jermaine Lau

For permission requests, please contact the publisher at:
Mango Publishing Group
2850 Douglas Road, 3rd Floor
Coral Gables, FL 33134 USA
info@mango.bz

For special orders, quantity sales, course adoptions and corporate sales, please email the publisher at sales@mango.bz. For trade and wholesale sales, please contact Ingram Publisher Services at customer.service@ ingramcontent.com or +1.800.509.4887.

The Academic Hustle: The Ultimate Game Plan for Scholarships, Internships, and Job Offers

Library of Congress Cataloging
ISBN: (p) 978-1-63353-933-4 (e) 978-1-63353-934-1
Library of Congress Control Number: (Library of Congress Cataloging-in-Publication has been applied for.)
BISAC category code: STU031000 STUDY AIDS / Financial Aid

Printed in the United States of America

Speaking engagements and bulk book orders

Email: info@theacademichustle.com

Website: www.TheAcademicHustle.com

This work was supported by the following Patrons of Matthew A. Pigatt: Valerie Pigatt, Randon Campbell, Michole Washington, Samiya Johnson, Jasmine Johnson, Stephanie Fortune-Branch, KeTia Harris, Jefferson Noel, Gaphna Mayard, Darrick Brown, Alexis Vidot, Kendra Marchal, Brian C. Johnson, Shaunna Gunter, Shelia Belzince, Licson Alfred

Become a Patron: www.patreon.com/matthewpigatt

Table of Contents

Part III: The Two Costs

Part IV: Putting It All Together

To My People

Acknowledgments

This book would not exist if it were not for my MamaLove, Valerie Pigatt. Her determination to graduate from college and provide a better life for her boys is the reason this book was developed. She was the first to get a degree in our family. MamaLove maxed out everything she had to secure the loans for my first two years at a premier private institution. She wanted me to be the first in the family to have a "real" college experience. If we would have had the information in this book, MamaLove and I may have been almost as awesome as my lil brother, Randon Campbell.

Randon was the guinea pig for *The Academic Hustle*™. One of the highest honors of my life is having a lil brother who listens, appreciates, and respects me. He constantly inspires me to be a better person. Randon earned over $250,000 in scholarships for his undergraduate degree, and $80,000 to attend the University of Michigan School of Dentistry, the #1 dental school in the world. He is taking our family's legacy to the next level with a dentist's salary! That is the purpose of this book, to teach people how to get paid while making our family and community proud.

My grandfather, Melvin Pigatt, was the patriarch of the family. He is responsible for my hustler mentality. I have a huge family and hustling runs deep in our lineage. Over twenty-nine aunties and uncles. Almost everyone has their own squad of kids with unique hustles. For me, it was academics and career development.

I owe it to the men of the 100 Black Men of South Florida for pulling my head out the gutter, even when my mouth spat sewage at anyone who tried to give me helpful advice. Mark Valentine saved my life. He always believed in me and even gave me my first office job. He had this beautiful waterfall in the office and it was my job in the mornings to open and get it started. I would regularly and unintentionally flood his office. I drove my first luxury vehicle, a BMW, while running errands for him.

Glendon Hall has become the father I never had. In every major step of my life, Glen has been there to assist in ways only a man of love and wisdom can. The 100 Black Men of South Florida and Glen, through The Morehouse Alumni Association of Broward, awarded me my first scholarships.

Dear old Morehouse…the place that made me into the man I am today. I could write a book about what Morehouse has taught me…well, another book. All the experiences mentioned throughout the pages of this book are credited to my time at Morehouse. I entered Morehouse full of "hood" arrogance, and Morehouse showed me so many examples of Men of Excellence that I could not help but to reevaluate myself and my standards. Men like Dr. Marcellus Barksdale, the founder of the African American Studies Department at Morehouse College, were among the pillars of men who I would run up against over and over again. My stubborn, arrogant, and disrespectful attitude were chipped away each time. I licked the wounds to my self-esteem and grew into a better man. It was Morehouse that molded me and I am forever true.

To everyone who dismissed me: Thank you. The rage I felt after being belittled fueled the late nights and early mornings. Those times ultimately led to my personal development. The many dark and lonely places where I cried out—all the thoughts and reminders that I was not good enough were replaced by an even stronger determination to prove people wrong. That fire burned away imperfections of spirit and refined me.

Finally, to those who made this book one of the most proudest things I ever done in my life, Thank you. It took over 10 years to produce. Thank you. John Peragine for organizing the original structure. Dr. William Hobbs for bringing my story to life. Kierra Bryant, Indra Campbell, Tyrionne Paul, and Antionette McCoy for the detailed line-by-line edits.

Shout out to the whole Mango Publishing Team! Ashley Blake for making the connection with Mango and putting this book on the map! Chris McKenney for believing in this work and signing me on the team. Yaddyra Peralta for editing the manuscript and being there with me every step of the process. Jermaine Lau for crafting such a beautiful manuscript and eye-catching cover. If this work is in your hands, then the marketing and logistics team, Michelle Lewy, Hannah Paulsen, and Hugo Villabona did their thing!!

What you hold in your hands are the lessons I learned through great personal sacrifice. Every tip, technique, and suggestion have a story of personal growth behind it. Through this book, you get to climb over my mountain of struggles and journey further. But, you still must climb, navigate your own path, and hustle.

Thank you for helping me improve my community (YOU) by reading this book, being an example of its teachings, spreading the world. Your support helps me eat, provide for my family, and accomplish my mission.

Thank you.

My Story (The Come Up Wasn't Pretty)

I'm from where the hustle determines your salary.
—Rick Ross

My mother was pregnant with me as she walked across the stage at Miami Northwestern Sr. High for her diploma in 1986 and, at that time in South Florida, that was considered to be a crowning achievement. Although she was already a young mother (my older brother was three years old at the time), my mother didn't see it that way.

As the youngest daughter of fourteen siblings, my mother became the first and only in the family to attend college. During her freshman year, while living on campus at a local college, she had to withdraw to raise her two boys as a single mother.

Growing up, I thought she had dropped out of college. When mentioning that one day, I had to maneuver to escape a smack on the head for making such an assumption. You see, when my mother left her first college, Florida Memorial University, she continued her studies but reduced her course load and always took at least one course each semester. She was still in it to win it. After twelve years and four colleges, she became the first person in the family to receive a college degree. I was in middle school at that time. Many thought that was her crowning achievement, the jewel of her testimony, that she had arrived, and, that Ms. Valerie Pigatt could finally sit her stubborn, educated self down somewhere… but, she did not stop there.

She went on to get her CPA license and master's degree in business administration. It took many years and different schools, but she did it while working to raise not two, but now three boys on her own. That's right, three.

If you're reading this book, chances are you're past the knucklehead mentality I was in at that time. You've (hopefully) abandoned the "mediocre is cool" mentality. I was in middle school at the time and paid no attention to Mama's struggles and achievements. We were a low-income family, and my mother worked through stretches of days that allowed only four hours of sleep, bills seemed to come from every direction, and broken promises to take us beyond our circumstances flooded our household. While she lost touch with friends who lived in the clubs to pursue her dreams and keep a roof over our heads, I hung out with friends in the streets and did just enough to get by in school.

The realization that I needed to do something with my life did not hit me until I was in the in the second half of 11th grade. By that time, I had a 2.1 cumulative Grade Point Average (GPA). It was not that I was dumb. Like many males of color, I just did not care about school. To fit in, I skipped class and hung out. I did not see the usefulness of school when I was able to make money instead; however, I had a rude awakening.

During that 11th grade year, reality hit as I sat in a courtroom facing felony charges. As I sat in the courtroom, I tried to brace myself for life as a juvenile delinquent by replaying every Tupac song in my head. But over the next few weeks, I had to watch my mother go through fits of crying so hard, she would hyperventilate and couldn't keep food down. She would come home from work, put her purse down, go into her room, and collapse in the bed to weep while still in her work clothes.

My lil brother would cry, too. Not just because Mama was crying, but because he was already missing our older brother who had been incarcerated a few months prior. Yeah, it was like that. I wasn't bringing anything but headaches to the situation. At the time, I did not know any better. I would sit there in the house wondering why Mama was so hurt. Eventually, I approached her and asked what the big deal was. Why was she trippin'? People get locked up. People get put on probation. That's life (or more particular, the life of too many Black males in America). She propped herself up on her elbow and looked back at me with her mouth open in horror. I just knew I was going to get hit, so I backed up. She got to the edge of the bed with her eyes staring at my mouth in amazement. Her look shifted to anger as she sat at the bed's edge. She exhaled. Her anger turned into grave concern. Mama laid her forehead in the palms of her upturned hands and told me her story…

Right after having she gave birth to my brother at fifteen, a group approached my mother in her hospital room. They asked her personal questions and when those questions became invasive, she wanted to know their purpose. She was tired and just wanted to heal. They kept beating around the bush and she finally gave them an ultimatum: provide an answer or leave. They finally said they were performing a study on teenage pregnancy and wanted to know if those children would end up involved with the law.

My mother flipped. She pounded the hospital bed rail and demanded they leave. How in the world would they dare discuss her child going to jail immediately after his being born? Fuming, she vowed that that would never happen to her children. And yet, eighteen years later, two out of her three sons were in trouble with the law. She had done all she could by working and going to school to raise her sons out of the "hood," but it was not enough. She could not win against a justice system that targets, disproportionately arrests, and overly prosecutes Black males. And, most importantly, she could not win with children far too comfortable with living up to the world's low expectations.

After hearing that story, I realized I needed to do something with my life. My family was going through a lot and I wanted to put a smile back on my mother's face. Additionally, I could not stop worrying about my lil brother. What would he become without strong and successful male role models in his life? He already had two brothers who got involved with the law. To top it all off, getting caught up with the law costs money! Who would wind up having to pay? Oh no, I could not let that happen. My priorities shifted so deeply that I felt goosebumps.

Luckily, my mother came across a group called the 100 Black Men of South Florida, Inc., a local chapter of the national organization, the 100 Black Men of America. The 100 is a professional network of Black men dedicated to developing youth and empowering the African American community. The South Florida chapter had a group mentorship program now called the *Dr. Harold Guinyard Leadership Academy*. Knowing that we didn't have any strong male role models in our lives, my mother made sure her boys were in the program. Almost every other week I attended a group mentoring session with prosperous Black male professionals. The sessions involved twenty to thirty boys and about five to seven Black men—laywers, judges, financial advisors, and other high-ranking officials. At the time, I viewed them as old men who talked WAY TOO MUCH! In addition, I thought they were stuck up and bougie. However, when my priorities changed, I began to look at them differently.

The men of the 100 drove nice cars, had big houses, and, most importantly to me, made money. My father was not in my life, and I had no concept of what it meant to be a successful, professional man. Many of the men in my community and family barely had their own place to stay. However, these men of the 100 were on point. I was not only blessed with the opportunity to see them, but also had the chance to get to know them and their families. This may seem small to you, but at the time, I did not know any Black, professional men. I kept wondering why? What made them different? Looking at the men of the 100, the men in my family and the community, the only difference I could find was that all the men of the 100 went to college and none of the men in my family or community that I knew ever did. That is when I realized there had to be something valuable to this college stuff, and so I vowed to attend and graduate just like my mother.

During my senior year, I got straight As and one B+. It was actually pretty easy: I stopped feeding into distractions, which allowed me to focus on what was most important. That meant showing up to class, taking tests seriously, and completing all my assignments. That's it. In addition, my classes were not rigorous. Think about it: Is it really that hard to get an A in a class? Not really. The biggest problem most people have is being strong enough to cut their your so-called "friends" who don't respect their grind. In this regard, I did not have to exert myself too much to get an A. But because of my late start in taking school seriously, I graduated with a 2.7 cumulative GPA (which was barely enough to get into college). That low GPA meant I lost out on all kinds of scholarships. Luckily, the 100 helped get me into Morehouse College, the premier institution for educating Black men in this world.

Morehouse College was my promised land. It is the alma mater of Dr. Martin Luther King Jr., Samuel L. Jackson, Spike Lee and other notable men. I had never before imagined so many Black men in college. These men weren't young men that hung on the street; instead they were the sons of politicians, celebrities, lawyers, and businessmen from all walks of life. I was surrounded by national speech champions, valedictorians, salutatorians, Gates Millennium Scholars, and so many others with distinctions. Here I was thinking how awesome I was compared to my peers for leaving my home state to attend college, and I was surrounded by award-winning, world-traveling young men with family lineages of distinction. I needed to step my game up. WAY UP.

That hopeful future, however, was not guaranteed. My money situation was crucial. When my mother dropped me off at Morehouse, her last words were, "*Baby, I hope you make the most of this because I can only do two years' worth of loans.*" While people back home blew their money and credit scores on cars, stereos, and clothes, my mother maxed out everything to invest in me. Everything. From time to time, I'd lean against a wall between classes from the very idea of it; my eyes would close, and I'd get warm in the face.

I needed to show respect for my mother's efforts by getting cash money lined up for the rest of my years at Morehouse. It was as simple as that; I had to do something to secure the funds to finish school. On top of that, I entered on academic probation, which meant that if I failed one class, I would be kicked out. There I was at the top school in the world for men of color. I was surrounded by opportunity and amazing people I never even imagined existed. This was my chance to fulfill my mission of putting a smile on my mother's face and becoming a role model for my lil brother. I knew that if I did not make it at Morehouse, there would be no hope for me. I would have probably ended up back on the streets, which may have led to being locked up like my older brother. So, I turned to what I knew and made college my hustle.

Over the next five years in college (yes, I stayed an extra year. Why not? I was in no rush to get into the "real world." Not to mention, I got someone else to pay for it!), I earned over $100,000 in scholarships, fellowships, and awards that took me all over the nation and paid for my international travels. As I became a high-achiever, I wondered what made me, the men of Morehouse, and the men of the 100 distinctive? Was it luck? Was it hard work alone? Or was it networking with the right people?

When I got to go to Emory University and the University of California-Berkeley for research programs, I decided to figure out how great Black men developed despite the odds. What books did they read? What did they do differently from others? What were the factors that led to their success? I made it my mission to find the answers, so I could take it back to my family and community. I continued to develop the research over years and eventually won a few national awards for it.

I distilled what I learned from my personal transformation and my national award-winning research into a system. After returning to Morehouse, I began to teach this system and went on to expand it in the surrounding schools. After seeing impressive results in the young students, I took a chance and used my system with my lil brother. It paid off: he was accepted into Morehouse College with about $250,000 in scholarships. A lot of guys with both our backgrounds barely make it into college. The smallest hiccup with paying tuition or any small obstacle can have them dropping out and unloading stock at Walmart, hoping for something to save them. Let me repeat: my brother was accepted into Morehouse College with over $250,000 in scholarships. He's getting his education with plenty of money because I taught him how to hustle. At the time of this writing, my lil brother, Randon Campbell, is in his first year at the University of Michigan Dental School; the #1 dental school in the WORLD with over $80,000 in scholarships. I recognize that I am relatively young to have come across and shared what I have discovered and that's a good thing. It proves that you don't have to wait to be 40-something to make moves. In this book, for the first time, I have laid out that system. This is how you can become a high-achiever and GET PAID NOW, while achieving your dreams. This is the promise of *The Academic Hustle.* Let's get it!

The best things you get out of life require struggle.
If it don't, you gettin hustled homeboy.
You gettin hustled.
How I see it,
anything you wanna be you can be it.
—**Dead Prez, "The Game of Life"**

Introduction to The Academic Hustle

Hustle - To have the courage, confidence, self-belief, and self-determination to go out there and work it out until you find the opportunities you want in life.
—UrbanDictionary.com

Many people believe that to make money you have to be established in a career. I prefer to make money now. This book details the system I discovered as I was trying to get paid while still in school.

The Academic Hustle is about grinding and getting paid *now,* as in sending-an-email-or-fine-tuning-your-résumé-while-this-book-is-open-and-next-to-the-keyboard now. It is a systematic approach to earning money *while* developing a career. You can become a competitive candidate for any school, program, scholarship, or job by applying this system to your life. It is organized around the following concepts: Three Fundamental Truths, The Foundation, Four Pillars, and Two Costs.

Three Fundamental Truths

There are Three Fundamental Truths about making money in this world:

1. Money is exchanged for value

"For the Love of Money" by The O'Jays is classic R&B. My uncles would sit around at family gatherings sipping on Millers while that song played. They would reminisce about friends that had gone mad chasing money in vain, only for it to end with them either in jail or dead. With so many lives lost and ruined in pursuit of money, it is very easy to assume it is the answer to all things. It seems impossible to convince those who've never had it

that money isn't everything. Before we go any further, let's put its true value in perspective.

Money is simply a medium of exchange – period. It has no value outside of what we place on it. Most of us desire money because of the things we can get in its exchange. Some things such as friendship, love, and loyalty lose integrity and value when one attempts to gain them in exchange for money. Nevertheless, many are impressed with the respect and attention money can bring their way. It is not the physical money that we seek, but the options and value we can gain by acquiring it.

Throughout our lives, we constantly exchange money for the things we value, whether it is clothes, food, or cars. On both ends of the exchange, we are usually giving more value to the other person. For example, when you pay for a shirt, you are receiving something you can wear and feel good in. You pay money for that shirt because you believe the value you get out of wearing it is worth more than (or equal to) the price. You can wear it repeatedly for this one-time payment. By the same token, the retailer has secured that shirt at a discount and is selling it to you at a premium to maintain their business and make a profit. It is a win-win situation.

The same goes for someone who is giving money. People value the act of giving or helping someone else out. Many people feel satisfied knowing that they played a part in aiding a cause or person in need. Others enjoy being seen by others as a person of power and influence. Many will drop a few dollars in the bucket for the Salvation Army, give a twenty-dollar bill to a Girl Scout for a box of cookies and tell them to keep the change, or write a check to create scholarships in their church. When one gives and documents it, there is also the bonus of getting a reduction in how much one pays in taxes to the government while being charitable.

On the other hand, when earning money, someone is exchanging money for the product or service you provide. Employers pay their employees for the value they produce. Scholarship committees are awarding money to people they believe are valuable to their mission, organization, or department. When money is involved, there is always an exchange occurring.

2. Value is determined by people

People determine what is valuable. As a collective, society has placed value on money as the primary source of exchange. If we were to take that same currency of money to another group of people in another country, it will most likely not have the same power or value.

We determine what is valuable to us. Some of us value cake, while others value fruit. Some of us value going to the movies, while others value hiking. Some of us will pay hundreds of dollars for shoes, while others will spend that on a new phone. The value of something depends on whom you're talking to in that moment and their perception.

Employers and scholarship committees are no different; they have a set of skills, qualities, and experiences they value more so than others. If you want to get that job, scholarship, or fellowship, you must understand what the selection committee values and show that you value the same.

3. People are human

All companies, organizations, and institutions are run by people. People no different than you and me make the decisions to hire, promote and award scholarships. Your teachers, bosses, and colleagues are all human. It can be difficult to remember that when titles and protocols get thrown around. Trust and believe that the seemingly well put together person on the other side of the desk has family issues and drama with their friends. They like to joke, have fun, and spend far too much time on their phones while on the toilet. Just like you and me, they have likes, dislikes, and judge others based upon their own perspective. We naturally like some people more than we like others. We have our favorites and we have those who irritate us to no end, simply because they're breathing in the same room as we are. It is neither right nor wrong; it is just the way we are. We determine what is good and what is valuable based upon what we like.

When interacting with a supervisor, professor, or colleague, it is critical to remember that they are just as human as you are. Despite our age differences, we have the same basic desires, which are to feel appreciated and respected. We want what we want. We want what *we* value. And that is the key to success: give people what *they* want.

The sum of all these truths is this: **If you want to earn money in this world, increase your value in the eyes of the people with money.** That is the core of *The Academic Hustle*. It is a system designed to increase your value in the eyes of the businesses, institutions, and organizations to influence them to hire and award you scholarships.

The Foundation

There is more money in this world than there are people. Although there are millions of ways to make money, not everyone can take advantage of everything. You cannot be everything, however, you can become anything you want. The key to having the ability to make money is focus; identify what it is you truly want, then go from there.

The foundation of *The Academic Hustle* is in identifying what you want and why you want it. If you want to make sure you get to a specific destination, you must chart a path to get there. It is a very simple concept but too many of us are clueless about what we want out of life, where we want to go, or who we want to become.

We yearn for what we want but rarely take the time to figure out what it really is. Many fear cutting off options that could be profitable. It's hard for some to make a concrete decision and have tunnel vision on their path. In turn, they miss the countless possibilities that they are unable to see from a distance. It's time to get focused. Indecision will never attract money or the confidence of those who have it to work with you. This is the first step in *The Academic Hustle*. We must identify what we want.

Ask yourself: What are your career goals? What type of life do you want to live? What do you want to study in school? How much money do you need to pay for school (be realistic with yourself)? What school do you want to get into? What program do you want to be a part of? Once you know what it is that you want, you can figure out how to make it happen.

Knowing what you want is only half of the equation. There needs to be a strong reason or need to be fulfilled—beyond money—that will motivate you to get it. That deep motivating WHY will push you through all the obstacles that will inevitably cross your path. As a matter of fact, having a strong WHY is all you really need! If you are determined to get what you want no matter what, you will figure out what you must do.

Identifying **what you want** and **why you want it** sets the foundation for you to build yourself into who you need to become to get what it is that you want. This is extremely important, so much so that I'm going to say it again – ***Identifying what you want and why you want it sets the foundation for you to build yourself into who you need to become to get what it is that you want.*** It narrows your focus and helps you determine what you need to do to become valuable in the eyes of the people who have your money.

Four Pillars

The Four Pillars are your guiding posts. These are the areas you must develop to become a competitive candidate for the opportunities you are going after. In just about every opportunity you pursue, the employers or selection committees are going to examine you in these four areas to determine your value:

1. What do you know? Your **Education**
2. What have you done? Your **Experience**
3. What do people say about you? Your **Relationships**
4. What do you say about yourself? Your **Presentation**

Your mission is to identify what are the most valuable answers to these questions in the eyes of the selection committee. Once you have the answers to these questions, *strategically develop yourself* into the ideal candidate in those areas.

As with all things, there is a balancing act. You will be strong in some areas and weak in others. This is a part of being human.

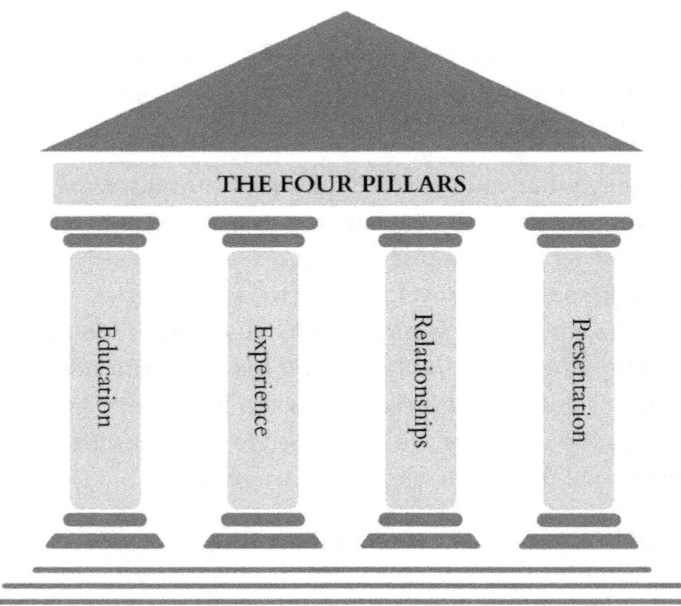

Ensure that your weaknesses are compensated by your strengths. However, this should never take away from the fact that you must do what you must do to mold yourself into the ideal candidate in each of these areas. These are the pillars of your professional life. You must continuously develop in each of these areas. It NEVER stops. There is never a time to go on autopilot with your career. You have to be that person people trust within the industry. This isn't going to be a problem if you truly love what it is that you do. You must invest time into updating yourself and improving in any area that is a weakness for you.

Two Costs

Once you know what it is that you want and why you want it, then you must invest your time and money into developing the Four Pillars in that area. Nothing will happen unless you invest your time and money into it. Put your money, your time, and yourself out there. When it comes to this, "scared living ain't living." It is a thief of time.

Time is of the essence and our most precious resource. It is the only thing that we can never get back or replay. Everyone has the same 24 hours daily. It is what we do with those 24 hours each day that develops us into athletes, professionals, or bums on the street. Your success is based upon how you invest your time. If you are careful about your time and invest it into the Four Pillars of what you want, you will eventually achieve your goal.

Everything costs. As you invest your time, you will inevitably have to manage your costs. Having a sound understanding of the expenses related to your goals and managing your money to make sure you achieve them is critical to success.

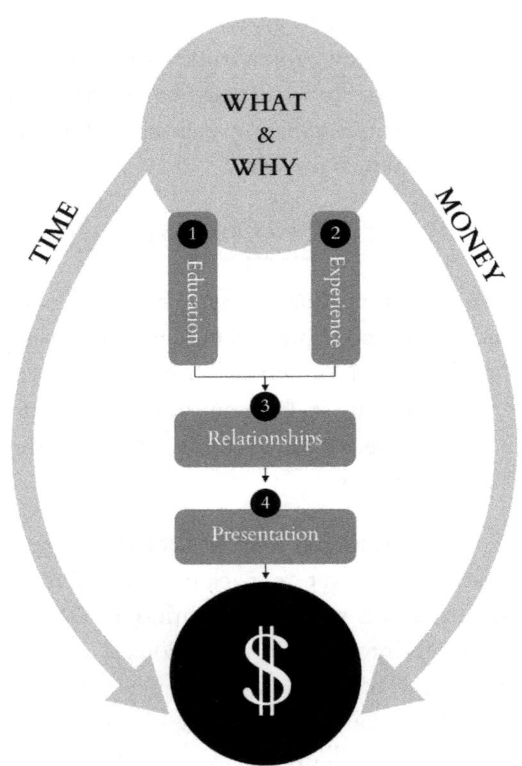

If you do not read anything else in this book, know this:

1. Make it your top priority to clearly identify what you want and why you want it.

2. Understand what type of education you need to attain your goals. Strategically pick classes that are interesting, challenging, and will further your goals. Strive to get an A in every class.

3. Get involved on and off campus. Do things that you enjoy and/or will set you up for your next step. Focus on developing an impressive résumé.

4. Be intentional about making great impressions on everyone you meet. Be strategic about cultivating good relationships with people who can help you develop into who and what you want to be, write strong recommendation letters, and who can be a good reference.

5. Tailor how you present yourself as the ideal candidate for every opportunity you go after.

This is the heart and soul of *The Academic Hustle.* A motto worth remembering is: STRATEGICALLY FOCUS ON WHAT YOU NEED TO DO IN ORDER TO ACHIEVE YOUR GOALS. If you want to ensure that you are never without opportunities, then continue to develop and always plan your next step.

To get the most out of this book, complete each exercise. They build upon each other, which means they are more effective if completed chronologically. For more insight and resources, check out the website:

www.TheAcademicHustle.com

Life is not about the quickest speed.
What you achieve
come degree by degree.
And what you get is what you see
in your mind visually
and manifest physically.
*If you stick to it sh*t'll*
work out terrifically.
—**Dead Prez, "The Game of Life"**

Do You Need The Academic Hustle?

As you can see from my story, I was headed for trouble. I had no idea of what I could achieve and, therefore had no focus. To help you get the most out of this book, complete the following assessment with the utmost honesty. While I encourage you to read every section, the answers to the questions below will help you fine-tune your focus.

Setting the Foundation

It all starts with knowing where you want to go and why…

1. Do you know what you want out of life?

    a. No idea.

    b. I have thought about it.

    c. I have a good idea.

    d. There are a few things I want.

    e. I know exactly what I want.

2. Do you have a reason that impels you to do whatever it takes to get what you want?

    a. No.

    b. I think so.

    c. I have a reason, but it doesn't impel me to do everything.

    d. Yes.

    e. Yes, there is nothing that will stop me.

3. Do you have an idea in which field you intend to work?

    a. I have no idea.

    b. I have thought about it.

    c. I have a few jobs/careers I am looking into.

    d. I have narrowed it down to 2–3.

    e. I know exactly what I want to do in life.

4. Have you identified what steps you need to take to get to your dream job?

    a. What do you mean?

    b. No.

    c. I have an idea.

    d. I have a general plan.

    e. I know exactly what I need to do.

5. Do you know why you want to go into a certain career?

    a. No.

    b. Not really.

    c. Yes, I have a general idea.

    d. Yes, I am clear on my reasons for choosing my career.

    e. Yes, and my reasons are why I will do whatever it takes.

6. Do you write goals for yourself?

    a. No.
    b. I have a few in my head.
    c. I've done it before.
    d. For major things in my life.
    e. All the time… and I make sure they are S.M.A.R.T.

    Are you constantly reminded of your goals daily?

    a. I don't have goals.
    b. I think about them from time to time.
    c. I have them written somewhere.
    d. I review my written goals from time to time.
    e. Yes, I review my written goals multiple times a day.

Education

I was told education is about teaching people how to think. I had to bump my head a few times to see what that meant. Here are some questions to better assess where you are concerning your education.

1. Is your institution or school's department the right environment for you to develop?

    a. I am not in school.
    b. I go just to get my degree.
    c. It has my major.
    d. Yes, it is one of the best schools for my field.
    e. Yes, my department, people, and opportunities fit me perfectly.

2. Are your passions, interests, or strengths the main factor in your choice of a major?

    a. No.

    b. I am doing it for the money or because some else said it is a good idea.

    c. Sort of… It is interesting.

    d. I think I will enjoy it.

    e. I LOVE MY MAJOR! THIS IS WHAT I WAS BORN TO DO!

3. Are you taking classes that will prepare you for the industry in which you plan to work?

    a. No.

    b. I believe that is why my advisor picked my classes.

    c. I think so.

    d. Duh! That is the point of college, right?

    e. Yes, my classes align with career goals.

4. Outside of your requirements for graduation, are you taking classes that you enjoy?

    a. I am not in school.

    b. My classes are boring.

    c. My classes are okay.

    d. I am somewhat interested in them.

    e. I love my classes.

5. Do you maintain a 3.3 or higher GPA?

    a. Uh, no. Less than a 3.0

    b. 3.0 - 3.3

    c. 3.3 - 3.5

    d. 3.5 - 3.7

    e, 3.7 - 4.0

6. Are you implementing a system to manage your time?

    a. No.

    b. I know the important things I have to do.

    c. I usually have an idea of what I need to do.

    d. I use an agenda and make to-do lists when I need to.

    e. I write down my tasks and use an agenda daily.

7. How would you describe how you organize yourself for class?

    a. What do you mean?

    b. I know where everything is.

    c. I try to stay organized.

    d. I have a folder for each class.

    e. I keep my notes, handouts, assignments, and anything else related to class in place and ready.

Experience

Books alone will not do, so…

1. Are you in, or planning to be on, the executive board of an organization?

   a. I don't do stuff like that.

   b. I am thinking about it.

   c. If I am selected, I will.

   d. If that is what it takes to get ahead.

   e. Definitely.

2. Are you involved in a club that will prepare you for your career?

   a. No.

   b. Still trying to figure it out what my career will be.

   c. Yes, I am involved in one.

   d. Yes, I am involved in a few organizations that expose me to a couple of my career options.

   e. Yes, I am also on the executive board of one.

3. Are you involved in an organization that does things you enjoy doing?

   a. No.

   b. Haven't found one yet.

   c. Yes.

   d. Yes, I am involved in a few.

   e. Yes, I am also on the executive board.

4. Do you regularly attend events and conferences?

    a. No.

    b. Only when I must.

    c. Yes.

    d. Yes, I am trying to take advantage of everything this place has to offer.

    e. Yes, I look for events, take notes, and network.

5. Are you strategic about whom you network with?

    a. What? I can get money?!

    b. If you tell me about them, I will try to get into one.

    c. I have my eyes set on one.

    d. Yes.

    e. Yes, and they are preparing me for my career goal.

6. Are you participating in any programs during your summer break?

    a. No.

    b. I may get a job, most likely one that is not focused on developing my career.

    c. If the right opportunity presents itself, I will.

    d. There is one program I am looking into.

    e. Of course, I have a few programs I am applying to.

7. Do you have any honors or awards?

    a. I never win any awards.

    b. I won a minor one that doesn't have anything to do with professional development.

    c. Yes, I have one that will look good on my résumé.

    d. I have a few.

    e. Why yes, I have quite a few, actually.

Relationships

This is one of the most overlooked aspects of becoming successful. People who step up their game do so with, help from others.

1. Do you purposefully try to create a pleasant impression on everyone you meet?

    a. No.

    b. When I am in the mood.

    c. Only certain people I like.

    d. I just try to be nice.

    e. Yes. I never know who might be a blessing.

2. Are you intentional about building relationships with faculty and staff?

    a. Never.

    b. When I have to.

    c. When I need a favor or a break.

    d. Every now and then.

    e. I make an effort to develop strategic relationships.

3. Are you good at small talk?

    a. I don't like talking to people.
    b. No.
    c. I can do it with friends or family.
    d. Yes, I am okay.
    e. Yes, I can talk to anyone.

4. Do you have faculty and staff who look out for you on campus?

    a. No one knows me on campus.
    b. Someone may do something kind for me randomly.
    c. Yes, there is someone who makes sure that I am doing well.
    d. I have a few.
    e. I have quite a few people look out for me on campus.

5. Are you strategic about with whom you network?

    a. Networking? What is that?
    b. If they are near me I may speak.
    c. I give a few people my cards.
    d. I try to make at least one contact at each event.
    e. I identify key people and make sure they know me.

6. How many people do you know will write you a strong recommendation?

    a. No one will.

    b. I think someone might, maybe.

    c. I have 1-2 people.

    d. I have a few people.

    e. As many as I might need.

7. Do you usually stand out in a good way in class or activities?

    a. No, I'm usually at the back of the class in my own world.

    b. I pay attention.

    c. I ask questions and participate every now and then.

    d. I usually participate during class and events.

    e. Of course, I almost always ask questions, participate and am engaged.

Presentation

How you step to people is (almost) everything…

1. Do you research every opportunity to which you apply?

    a. Research? What do you mean?

    b. No.

    c. Sometimes.

    d. No, only my top choices.

    e. Yes, it is the first step before applying.

2. How do you research your opportunities?

    a. Conduct an online search about it.

    b. Visit their website.

    c. Talk to people who are connected to the opportunity.

    d. Collecting notes from various sources.

    e. All the above.

3. Do you tailor all your application materials to the opportunity you are going after?

    a. What do you mean by tailor?

    b. No, I don't have time for that.

    c. Sometimes I change a few things here and there.

    d. Some of the materials, but not all.

    e. Yes, every application I submit is tailored to the opportunity's desires.

4. Do you have an elevator speech?

    a. What is that?

    b. No.

    c. Something like that. I have a few things I normally say to people.

    d. Yes, I have a well-practiced one.

    e. Yes, and I tailor it to each situation.

5. Do you speak their language (the jargon of that specific industry) when presenting yourself to an opportunity?

    a. Huh?

    b. I just tell them that I am a great person.

    c. I tell them what I have done in the past.

    d. I use stories to illustrate the points I am making.

    e. Yes, I practice telling stories of my experiences using their language.

6. Do you have a system for putting together and submitting applications?

    a. No.

    b. I just submit the application when I am done.

    c. I do what they say and turn it in.

    d. Yes, I have an order to how I submit applications.

    e. Yes, I have a checklist to ensure I submit a high-quality application on time.

7. How would you rate your writing skills on a scale of 1 to 5?

    a. 1-Poor.

    b. 2-Fair.

    c. 3-Good.

    d. 4-Great.

    e. 5-Awesome.

Time

Time is the most precious resource in life. It is life, itself…

1. How well do you manage your time?

    a. I don't.

    b. Horribly.

    c. Okay.

    d. Good.

    e. Great.

2. Do you have an agenda?

    a. No.

    b. In my head.

    c. I have sketched out my general timeframe for the week.

    d. I have a routine.

    e. Yes, an agenda I follow daily.

3. How do you organize all the things you have to do?

    a. I don't.

    b. I am trying to figure that out.

    c. I write things down.

    d. I write them down, review and prioritize.

    e. I have a system I developed.

4. Do you carry your agenda around with you?

    a. I don't own one.
    b. No.
    c. I take it sometimes.
    d. No, but I make sure I write down what I must do the first chance I get.
    e. I take it everywhere I go.

5. Do you write down what you have to do?

    a. No.
    b. I make a mental note.
    c. Sometimes.
    d. For major tasks.
    e. Yes, almost everything.

6. Do you have and maintain a calendar of all the things you must do for class and for your involvement in other organizations?

    a. No.
    b. I know what I have to do in my head.
    c. Yes, it has all the major dates.
    d. Yes, I reference it every now and then.
    e. Yes, I update it at least weekly or when I have a new class or project.

7. Do you prioritize?

    a. No.

    b. I just do what I have to do.

    c. Sometimes.

    d. Yes, I make sure I get the major tasks completed.

    e. Yes, I have a system.

Money

You know this book is about making money, right?

1. How would you rate your knowledge on managing your personal finances?

    a. Not good.

    b. Okay.

    c. Good.

    d. Great.

    e. Excellent.

2. Do you have a budget you follow?

    a. No.

    b, I know when I am spending too much.

    c. I know how much not to spend.

    d. I am careful about what I spend.

    e. Yes.

3. Do you track your income and expenses?

    a. No.

    b. I know when I have money and when I don't.

    c. Sometimes.

    d. Only when I am running low on funds.

    e. Yes, every purchase.

4. Do you know the main ways you can get money to pay for school?

    a. No.

    b. I am trying to get scholarships.

    c. I know a few.

    d. I believe so.

    e. Yes, I've studied quite a bit on how to pay for school.

5. Do you know the exact cost to go to school each semester?

    a. No.

    b. I have an idea.

    c. I know how much tuition costs.

    d. I know how much all the standard fees are.

    e. Yes, I know all the standard fees and have an estimate for books, supplies, and other costs.

6. Do you have a list of opportunities you plan to pursue?

    a. Opportunities for what?
    b. I know I need money for school.
    c. I have an idea of what I will be applying to.
    d. Yes, I'm just waiting on you to tell me how.
    e. Yes, and I have already started to develop my application materials.

7. What is the main way you identify the opportunities you go after?

    a. I don't know how.
    b. I use popular scholarship and job databases.
    c. Looking at postings around campus.
    d. Through the relationships I have developed.
    e. Through people in my department or activities I am engaged in.

Using the following key, calculate your score by adding up your answers.

a = 1

b = 2

c = 3

d = 4

e = 5

What is your score for the following sections?

What & Why ______________

Education ______________

Experience ______________

Relationships ______________

Presentation ______________

Time ______________

Money ______________

Total ______________

If your score was below 21 in any section, concentrate on developing yourself in that area.

If your score was between 21 – 32 in any section, peruse that section to understand what you can do to improve.

If your score was above 33 in any section, then you may be able to skip that section in this book. However, you never know what you may learn to improve how awesome you already are.

If your total score was below 147, then this book is one of the best investments you have ever made. This book is for you. Be sure to read, take in, and apply everything.

If your score was between 147 – 234, then take the time to review this book and use it to improve yourself.

If your total score was higher than 235, then congratulations!!! Money and opportunities are surely aligning themselves to your path. You are a force to be reckoned with. The sections on Tailoring your Presentation and Identifying Opportunities may of most value to you.

You have taken the first step to mastering *The Academic Hustle*! Continue to use this assessment as a guide to measure how well you are taking advantage of this system.

The Foundation of The Academic Hustle

If you know exactly what you want and are determined to achieve it, all you have to do is put in the work.

Set The Foundation: Identify What and Why

Anything you wanna be you can be it
If your mind can perceive it
And your heart really believe it
Then you half way there and all you got to do is do it
And if you give it all you got there ain't really
Nothin to it
—Dead Prez, "The Game of Life"

This chapter's objectives are designed to:

- Help you figure out what you want out of life.
- Identify your motivation to do it.
- Create a plan for your career.
- Provide you with the tools to understand where you are.
- Define the steps to get you where you want to be.

Although life can be challenging, we are blessed to operate beyond the world of common animals that react based on mere circumstance. We must secure our basic needs for food, clothing, and shelter; however, we can also craft a life that will fulfill our needs, wants, desires, while realizing our dreams. Unfortunately, society is organized in a way that diminishes our unique and powerful individuality. We are socially and culturally brainwashed into being mindless consumers focused on clothes, likes on social media, money, and the latest goofy attitude or saying for the sake of popularity. The idea of looking into and understanding ourselves is considered "deep." We have such an unconscious fear of looking inside ourselves to uncover what truly inspires us because of what others may think. Living with this fear causes us to dismiss those who are on the journey into greatness. We become lazy spectators of life and view the work needed to realize our dreams as too draining because, honestly, we really don't feel we are worth it. "Oh well," we say. We choose what we thing are more important things to do and experience.

People on the path of discovery are on the move, even if they seem to be completely still and meditating; after all, they are inwardly moving toward something. Such movement draws excitement, just as inaction would attract the unambitious. When you understand what inspires you and why, you just do it. This shows others what you're about in your speech ("closed mouths don't get fed") and in your actions ("lazy hands don't count bread"). Such activity builds reputation. It attracts those with similar interests, those who link up with you to upgrade their own dreams. This attraction pushes the dead weight out of your life and can unlock your potential to attract money and other resources beyond your wildest imaginations.

Understanding what you want out of life and why you want it will give you a certain amount of focus in life that very few people have.

Find the Motivation: Personal Mission Statement

A man with money is no match against a man on a mission.
—Doyle Brunson

Your purpose must be established before you can be about the money. If you have lots of money but no true aim in life, then you have resources without direction. You attract nothing but a lazy entourage willing to kiss up to you to get at your money. That's a sad situation. A man such as Barack Obama, with little money and a mission, can inspire those with money, influence, and connections to make all kinds of things happen.

We all go through life with a need to do something fulfilling, something that can change the world, our community, our families, or ourselves. Some of us want to create new things or improve on what is already out there. Others want to make money, gain recognition, or just excel. Whatever it is, we want to be fulfilled by what we do. We want to be proud of our actions and creations, and we also want to make our friends and family proud. One of the most rewarding things you can do in life is find and pursue what fulfills you. It will give you the motivation to do whatever it takes to be the best at what you want to do.

As I said earlier, having long-term goals and a vision for my life were not considered cool when I was a teenager. It was only cool to mumble about life with friends. Having pride in my hood and the streets was a way of placing a romanticized veil over the misery, poverty, and neglect of my community. Making money illegally was a buck against the system, which built up our street cred. Being a Black male from a low-income community in South Florida kept me from seeing my future past high school. For many of us, our options for making money, being celebrated, and being successful are limited to three worn-out choices: becoming an athlete, an entertainer, or a hustler. My childhood dream was to become a wide receiver for the Dallas Cowboys. That dream came to an end when I seriously injured my knee in an epic touchdown play during my last year of Optimist (youth athletic league) football. My dreams of breaking into the big leagues (high school football at the time) were crushed. I then had dreams of becoming a rapper. But…that was in my sleep. I thought I had a speech problem as a child and knew I couldn't be big time. Therefore, I turned to the only other option I thought I had.

I didn't go into much detail about it earlier, but since you're this deep into it with me, I might as well – I smoked blunts and sold ganja. My teenage mind was focused on having money, being "The Man" among my friends, and impressing girls. I was pretty good at it, too. Between 14 and 16 years old, I was making more money than most kids my age. I was The Man. I was having fun. I had money, women, and plenty of ganja. Life was good, from what I could see. Then, as you may remember, I got caught up…

Yep, that was two days after my 16th birthday when I found myself in a courtroom hearing the felony charges against me. I was sentenced to living the rest of my childhood on probation with a 9:00 p.m. curfew. No more family gatherings, hanging out with friends, or going out at night to a movie.

My curfew also meant I could not go out without "prior approval." I was stuck at home a lot, and I became bored. A person can only play so many video games or watch TV (we had the extremely slow dial-up version of the internet, so that was not an option). My mother saw me and handed me the book that changed my life!

It was crazy…years later when conducting my national award-winning research, I asked Black men at the top of their career, "What was the most powerful book you've ever read?" The book that ranked right above the Bible was the same book my mother handed me: *The Autobiography of Malcolm X.* EVERY teenager should read that book, especially 16-year-old Black boys. It tells the story of a young man who hustled on the streets of Harlem, got locked up, and transformed into the most powerful Black leader of the 20th century. One of the most pivotal things he did to change himself was read. So, just like Malcolm X did when he was locked up, I started reading…and my life transformed...

I began to hang out in the library. I gobbled up books for breakfast, lunch, and dinner. I had books for snacks, too. It was crazy how much I was reading. I was not a book person. I thought I hated reading. I barely touched the books assigned in school and would fall asleep when I had to read. However, I found subjects that caught my attention, like the self-help genre. I was hooked! I could not stop feeding my desire to learn how to transform myself. I would put a book down after finishing it and feel my skin tingling. I was outgrowing a dislike for books. My mind would buzz with a wider range of thoughts and I felt myself changing.

I probably read almost every self-help book in the Broward County Public Library. The people at checkout desks called out to me when I came in like they were cashiers at the liquor store and I was the neighborhood wino. I was hooked, and my addiction taught me a powerful lesson: *If you can clearly identify what you want, have a strong motivating desire for why you want it, and decide to go after it no matter what, then put in the time to figure it out and make it happen.*

Figure Out WHAT You Want in Life

Figuring out what you want is a simple process. Oftentimes, many people have trouble with this because they have never taken the time to ask themselves these two questions:

1. What do I want out of life?

2. What will make me happy?

Continuously ask yourself these questions until you narrow down what resonates with you. Only you can identify what the right answer is. It will *feel* right. You may experience goose bumps, a tingling or indescribable energy, or just a feeling of "rightness." I promise you, there is nothing quite like it. When you find the answer, it will put a smile on your face, determination in your gut, and a desire in your heart. Suddenly, you will see the so-called friends you're killing yourself to be around as a waste of your time and energy.

Once you find that answer, try to put it in one sentence without any commas. It will take time to do so, time well-spent. At sixteen, my WHAT was the following:

> *To put a smile on my mother's face and become a role model for my lil brother.*

Initially, I did not know how I was going to do this. It was motivating, but I had no concrete goal or benchmark to reach for. I needed something to measure how well I was moving toward my goal on a day-to-day basis. Once I was exposed to college, I realized how I was going to do it: by being a fully funded, well-connected, college graduate. So, my WHAT statement became:

> *I want to go to college, so I can put a smile on my mother's face and become a role model for my lil brother.*

The more specific you are, the better. When I say specific, I mean a realistic goal that you can achieve. It will be even better if it is a career goal. However, this WHAT statement may change over time. Once I got to college, it was:

> *I will find the money to pay for school within two years or end up back home and in jail like my older brother.*

Once I found the money to pay for school, I became a little cocky with my goals:

> *I will become a professor and prove that I know what I am talking about.*

Write your statement. Let me repeat that: WRITE it down.

Most people will read those statements and still not write theirs down. They can't make the mental leap required to take their success seriously yet. That's fine; somebody must make up the crowd that follows your lead. Do not be like most people and end up lost in a horde of mediocrity. Writing out your goal helps you clarify what you want. In addition, it is the first impression of your goal in the world. Writing out your goals takes them from fantasies in your head to real-world expressions. It is the declaration to the world and the universe that you are not to be taken as a joke.

Once you do this, you will not be wondering what you are doing in life anymore. Those days of needing constant entertainment to escape the boredom of living without direction and goals are done. You will have direction that empowers you. The more specific you can be about what you want, the more clearly you can define your path and determine your direction.

Exercise F1.1 – Identify WHAT You Want Out of Life

Get a notebook, a few sheets of paper, or open a new text document on your computer or your phone. Reserve 15 – 30 minutes of free time, free from any distractions. Write at the top of the document two questions:

1. What do I want out of life?

2. What will make me happy?

Write down everything that comes to mind without any filter. Just keep writing. After you cannot write anymore (push yourself to think and write for at least 10 minutes), read everything. Listen to your intuition and your body. If any thought puts a smile on your face or gets you excited, put a circle around it. Review your circled responses and select the top three. Write those top three on another sheet of paper.

Identify Your WHY

Ok, you've figured out what the WHAT is. What you want to do and why you want to do it goes hand in hand. Your WHY is the motivating factor. It is the most important question of this book. If you have a strong WHY for what you want to do, then nothing can stop you. The saying, "where there is a will, there is a way" is powerfully true.

Think about it—who would you bet your money on:

1. The top fighter in the world who is going after $1 million in a fight

2. Or his opponent, who is an experienced fighter but is participating in the fight to win $100,000 to pay for a heart

transplant for his mother who, otherwise, only has two weeks to live?

I know I would bet on fighter number two. Why? Because he will go all out to win no matter what. If both of his hands are broken during the fight, he will use his legs, if his legs were broken he would use his elbows, if his… you get the picture. That is how strong your WHY must be. It must be so strong, you will do whatever it takes to achieve your WHAT.

My WHAT drove me to go from a 2.1 GPA for most of high school to making straight As and one B+ during my senior year, but my WHY got me through college. That's saying a lot about my WHY, because I had never written a paper over three pages and did not like to study. I did not do work outside of class. In addition, I did not completely understand or was not completely sold on the "college stuff." However, I knew that if I failed there, I would probably end up back home and locked up like my older brother. I had to succeed.

What about you? What drives you? What is the WHY behind your what? If, after reading my story, you feel as though you do not have a strong WHY for your WHAT, don't stress about it. You don't have to come up fatherless in some desperate situation with crime and death at every turn. Anyone who had to live through that kind of struggle and has any sense is not trying to glamorize it. It ain't cute.

If you do not have a strong WHY for your WHAT, then you may need to change your WHAT, that's all. If you are going to succeed, if you are going to achieve things you could have never imagined for yourself, then you are going to have a strong reason that compels you to do it "by any means necessary." Now when I say, "by any means necessary," it is with the caveat of nothing immoral, unethical, or illegal. Criminality, for the sake of being lazy and not playing the game is not excused and is not cool. This is your life, not some "thugged-out" crime drama where you walk out of some club dressed in all Black with guns in both hands in slow motion while the building blows up behind you. This is not Hollywood.

Finding a better WHY means you will listen to whoever you have to listen to, read whatever you must read, do whatever you have to do…no matter what.

To figure out your "WHY," look at your what and ask yourself, "Why do I want to do this?" Continue to ask yourself why until you find a reason that resonates with you. Write that down and look at your WHAT and WHY statements, then ask, "Am I willing to do whatever it takes to make this happen?" If you hesitate for a moment, or have any doubt, then you need to find a deeper why or change your what. If you say yes, then ask yourself WHY am I willing to do whatever it takes to make this happen? The first thing that comes to mind is your true WHY.

Most people's WHY is usually associated with the way they were raised, their family, or immediate community. They have a reason to change, improve, or stop something from happening. What is this for you? Why is your WHAT important to any of the above?

Do not try to think hard about it. It is usually immediately apparent. You think about it almost all the time. It is what brings you to tears, stirs something inside of you, and energizes you. This is what your WHY does: it motivates you to DO something when other people would just shrug their shoulders. When you think about your WHY and any of those things happen, then lock on to that. Keep asking yourself WHAT and WHY until you find a combination that gives you power.

Just like when you crystallized your WHAT, when you identify your "WHY," try to state it in one sentence. For example, what motivated me to do well in high school and accomplish so much in college was:

It is up to me; I am the only one in the family.

Simple as that. It was all on me. If I failed, my mother would be crushed, and my lil brother would not have any men in the family to show him a better life. So, I had to get As in every class and figure out a way to pay for school. Period.

My WHY stayed the same as my WHATs (see above) until school was paid for and I was achieving a bit of success. Then it became:

> *I must be the one to show, by example, my people (especially my lil brother and the men in my family and community), that since I can achieve greatness, so can they.*

That WHY picked me up when I was knocked down. I was made to feel out of place quite a bit while in college. The other boys thought I was "ghetto" or unintelligent because of my strong, fast-talking country Miami slang. Many people couldn't understand me. I'm groaning as I type this just reminiscing about how clueless I was about things. I did not know what Greek fraternities were; I did not know a lot of the "high" fashion brands (i.e. Banana Republic, Brooks Brothers, etc.), or even beverages like cappuccino.

It was like I was some "ghetto," stereotypical character from some sitcom who had warped into the real word. Once, I was in a group and a young man walked up. Everyone was excited to see him and asked him what he did over the break. He said he went to Beijing. He must have seen the confusion on my face because he looked at me and said "China."

I was like, "Oh!" I thought about it for a second and got excited. I jumped up and inquired, "Did you see Kung Fu in the streets?"

I proceeded to do a few Kung Fu moves and told him he didn't have to go way over there to see it because I could show him a little something right then. He, and everyone, looked at me like I was the dummy of the year. He said, "I was with the Model UN debating the inflation of the yuan." I looked dumbfounded. I didn't have the slightest idea what in the world he was saying.

Model UN? Inflation? Yuan? Again, he saw it on my face and said, "It's economics." I looked at him and the group who clearly thought it was hilarious, lowered my head, and walked away. Things like that were common. VERY common. Actually, sometimes things like that still happen. Luckily, I still let this fuel my WHY.

What is your WHY? I challenge you to figure it out before you go any further. It will sustain you through those face-melting embarrassments that would cause other people pack their bags and return to the comfortable ignorance and lack of ambition they know. It will dry your eyes when you outright, totally and utterly fail. It is the most important thing you can get from this book. It is most important thing to know in any endeavor you undertake.

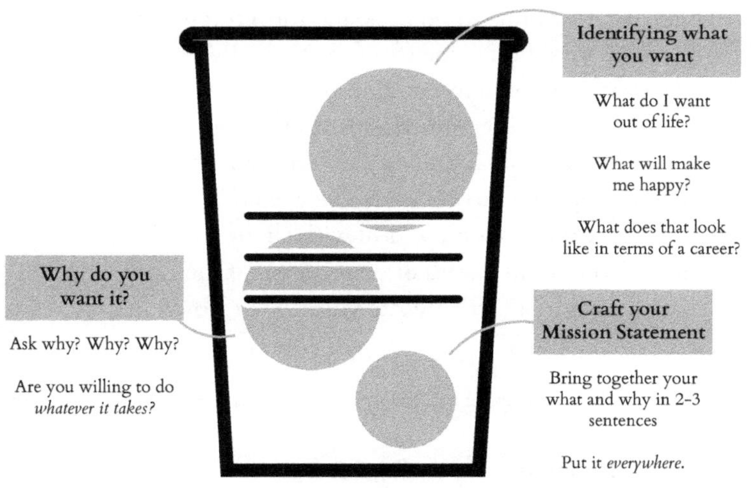

Exercise F1.2 – Identify a Strong WHY

Get a notebook, a few sheets of paper, or open a new text document on your computer or phone. Take at least 30 minutes of your free time, distraction-free. Write your three responses from Exercise 1.1 at the top of the document. Review those responses and ask yourself:

1. Why do I want this?

   Write what comes to mind. Take at least 5 minutes to ponder each response. Dig deep. Keep asking yourself "Why?" until you stumble upon an answer that stirs something in you. Once you arrive at that answer then ask yourself:

2. Am I willing to do *whatever* it takes to bring this into my life?

If you hesitate for even a moment, then rethink your WHAT. Redo Exercise 1.1 and then come back to this one. Continue to go back and forth through these exercises until you come to a firm YES, "by any means necessary" response to question two. Part of doing *whatever it takes* is completing ALL the exercises in this book. I may be smiling...but I'm serious! If your why doesn't impel you to complete these exercises, then it is not strong enough to deal with all the struggles of developing the career of your dreams. Once you have a strong one, then write your WHY down in a concise statement.

Develop a Personal Mission Statement

Once you have developed your WHAT and WHY statements, you must now engrave them in your heart and mind. That is why we are going to turn it into a personal mission statement. I am not talking about something grand, just 1-2 sentences that clearly articulate what you want and the primary motivating factor behind it.

Simply put the two statements you made above into a short paragraph. For example:

> *I must put a smile on my mother's face and become a role model for my lil brother. It is up to me. I am the one in the family that must succeed.*

You don't have to have anything "deep" or "powerful." It is all about what moves YOU. If your WHAT is a realistic goal that you can accomplish in life and your WHY is strong, then you have a personal mission statement. Another example,

> *I am an environmental activist because I am tired of seeing kids suffer from diseases caused by pollution.*
>
> *OR*
>
> *I witnessed my mother go through a bad marriage. I will become a family and marriage counselor to ensure that no one else have to go through what she and I went through.*

Write this down and put it where you can see it every day. Create a vision board. Infuse it into something in your life. For example, my mother's personal mission statement was:

> *I must go to college and become successful to create a better life for my children.*

Seeing her children every day reminded her of that mission.

Another point: you need a personal story behind that mission statement. The heart of your story lies within your WHAT and WHY. I really want to emphasize this point because once you identify your WHY, it will give you the motivation to figure out the WHAT and HOW. You won't *need* anything else. *If you have a strong enough WHY, nothing will stop you, not even yourself.* Take the time to figure out a clear idea of what you want and a very strong WHY you want it.

Here is a bad example of this exercise that most people will do.

I want to go to college to get a job, so I can take care of myself.

Now, if you have been homeless, abused in the foster care system, or been seriously hurt by not being able to take care of yourself then this may be a strong enough personal mission statement. However, if it is nothing that serious then this statement is childish, petty, and basic. Why? First, you don't need to go to college to get a job. Second, there is no specificity on the job. A goal like this leaves it open to getting any type of job, even one at a fast food restaurant. Third, the mission is selfish. WHYs are stronger when connected to others, *something bigger than your own immediate wants.*

Another example is:

I want to make a difference in this world.

I want to put a smile on my children's faces.

I want to make my parents proud.

These are all weak mission statements because they don't have a specific WHAT and, therefore, are pretty easy to accomplish. You can make a difference in this world by engraving your name on a freshly cemented sidewalk. You can play with your kids and see them smile. You can also do one thing to make your parents proud now.

Your personal mission statement must grow you into something that affects you now. It must be something specific that you can accomplish so there isn't any question that the mission is complete! If you shoot for the stars and slip up, then you will probably end up on the moon. If you really slip up, at least you will be in the sky. The point is you won't be on Earth with a bitter and broken fear to even look to the heavens. Shoot high!

I *strongly* encourage you to ALWAYS identify WHAT you want out of ANY situation and WHY you want it.

Exercise F1.3 – Create a Personal Mission Statement

Review your completed answers to Exercises 1.1 and 1.2. Combine them into 2-3 sentences that inspire you to get to work. When you write down those sentences you should feel a stirring inside: a pull, a yearning to accomplish what you write. If you do not feel it the first time, reword, rethink how you want to combine your WHAT and WHY. The final mission statement *may* not be an exact combination of your WHAT and WHY, but it should move you. Give yourself a week to hone your personal mission statement.

Once you have your personal mission statement completed, put it where you can see it daily. Write it on your bathroom mirror. Put it in your phone. Make or purchase something that symbolizes it and keep it on you or around you. Take the object and infuse it with the idea behind the mission statement. Be creative and put it where YOU know it will be a constant reminder of what you must do.

Determine Your Course: Career Planning

You may be asking yourself why is there a section on career planning in a book about school? At the end of the day, the reason you are investing your time and money into school is to learn something that will help develop your career. You are looking to be certified and apply what you learned to a job that will give you a long-standing return on your investment. Essentially, you are preparing yourself for your next step. Getting an idea of what your next step will be is crucial to ensuring that you are investing your time and money properly.

Know Yourself

Identifying a career starts with you.

1. What are your interests?
2. What are your skills?
3. What type of environment do you want to work in?

Going to school *just* to get a job, a better job, or any job is one of the worst decisions you can make in life. According to a 2012 article in *The Atlantic*, 53 percent of college graduates are either jobless or underemployed[1]. Therefore, if your goal is to *just* get a job or a better job then you have 50/50 chance of making that happen, even after four years of school.

If you attend school *just* to get away from your family and get a job, you will most likely spend a lot of money and waste a lot of time doing something that does not improve your life. The chances of you working a job you dread going to five out of the seven days of your week will be high. If you think about it, you've seen people who love what they do come home disgusted on occasion, although it's nowhere near the agony of people who hate what they do in general. If it is guaranteed that you will get annoyed from time to time in your career anyway, why not make it about something that you are inspired by and willing to fight for?

1 Weissmann, Jordan. "53 percent of Recent College Grads Are Jobless or Underemployed—How?" *The Atlantic*, http://www.theatlantic.com/business/archive/2012/04/53-of-recent-college-grads-are-jobless-or-underemployed-how/256237/. Accessed 6 April 2018.

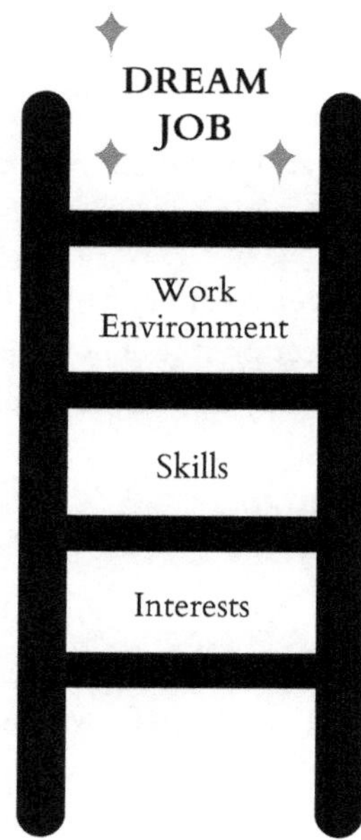

Get paid to do what you love.

Think about how you choose your mate. Relationships require a lot of work. Whoever you deal with is bound to irritate you at some point. Yet we pick the person who gives us more of what we want and in turn we deal with their negative traits.

Use the same logic with your career: go for what you love.

Doing what you love is good for you and your employer. When you love something, you care about it. You are more engaged in doing it well. Employers want engaged employees. They know that an engaged employee will perform better than others will[2]. Those employees will champion the company and make a good impression on customers.

Think about it. Which doctor would you want to operate on you?

2 "State of the American Workplace." *Gallup*, February 2017, http://www.gallup.com/services/178514/state-american-workplace.aspx.

1. One who doesn't care about your health but just wants a check?

2. One who loves what they do and will do everything in their power to make sure you get the best treatment?

Obviously, the right answer is number two. People who love what they do are usually better at it. They see their work as a reflection of themselves. They also want others to love what they love so they give their best.

The first step to figuring out your dream job is to identify your interests.

Exercise F2.1 – Identify Your Interests

Get a notebook, a few sheets of paper, or open a new word document. Take out at least 20 minutes of your time, distraction-free. Take your time and list *anything* and *everything* that has *ever* interested you.

Think back to when something caught your interest. Review childhood memories, interesting conversations, times where you had a lot of fun, or when you cared enough to learn more about something. Even if it was just a small inclination, write it down without a filter.

If you can't come up with at least 20 things, then you are thinking too hard about this exercise. Just list the things you like. This is *your* list of interests, not anyone else's.

Be honest with yourself when you identify your interests. Do not settle for things you are halfway interested in. Focus on the things that brighten your eyes—those that make you lose track of time. EVERY single thought or interest you have probably has an at least million-dollar industry behind it. To prove that point, look at your current environment right now. Try to find something that doesn't have a million-dollar industry behind it. The chairs, walls, floor, concrete, paper, the ink on this book—all of these things that make up your world were created by working people. Someone has dedicated their entire career to laying the foundation for your interests. You can develop it even more and get paid to do it!

Next, let's get an idea of your skills. Skills are the things you do well. The key here is to focus on the things you do well and enjoy doing. When you get a job, you will be doing things. Ideally, you want to spend as much time as possible doing the things you enjoy and do best.

Exercise F2.2 – Examine Your Skills

Get a notebook, a few sheets of paper, or open a new word document. Block out at least 10 minutes of distraction-free time. Write down your skills. All the things you do well. Think about what others have complimented you about. What work have you been proud of? What have you done that gave you a sense of accomplishment? What positive affect do you have on people, places, or things? Go back through the subject you were good in during school. What assignments did you do well? What were you involved in that made you feel good about your work?

Just list everything.

Another key component to finding your dream job is your environment. Figuring out the best environment to nurture your development is hard if you have not traveled much, held a few jobs, been involved in a few organizational activities, or experienced other people's workspaces. The more experience you have in a variety of work environments, the easier it is to determine the best one for you.

A work environment consists of the people, the workspace, timeframe, and geography. Take some time to figure out what works for you. Outside of your willpower, the environment is the greatest influence on your well-being and future. It is critical to be in an environment that contributes to developing who you want to be. No environment or group is perfect, but it is obvious when something either diminishes or contributes to what you are about. When someone realizes this and considers how much time they have wasted in toxic, unproductive situations, they get angry with themselves for letting it happen. Take that anger and transform it into energy toward finding the right environment.

Exercise F2.3 – Paint the Environment Where You Will Blossom

Sit back and dream. If you lived in the perfect world, where would you spend your working hours? Who would be the people you worked around? How would they treat you? Would you do most of your work on your own or with a team? How far would you have to travel for work? Where would your job be? Downtown? On the outskirts of town? At home? In a cubicle? Would you move around a lot?

Think back on all the environments where you have worked or have seen someone else work in. What did you like? What didn't you like? Get a sheet of paper and make a big T on it. On one side, list all the things you would want in a job environment and on the other list all the things you do not want in your job environment. List <u>everything</u>.

Once you have identified these things, you are ready to start narrowing down your career options. All of them are important because you can still be in a field you are interested in, but spending your time doing things you do not enjoy. Alternatively, you can do what you love to do but in an area that doesn't nurture your needs. However, if you are doing what you love and enjoy the atmosphere, then you have a winning combination.

Figure out Your Dream Job

Knowing your interests and passions sets the foundation for your dream job. Identifying the skills you want to apply, and the environment where these skills can blossom, narrows your dream job options. Now, all you must do is get to know the field your interests lie in, identify the types of jobs that exercise your best skills, and the companies or organizations that have the right environment for your life.

Specialized education, either through a college or trade/vocational program, is a good way to learn more about the fields that interest you. Indefinitely, the best way is by getting involved in the field, whether it is through a job, joining an organization, attending events, or volunteering. Getting involved in a field gives you hands-on experience with the people, environment, and types of work in your industry. Just watching interviews and video about someone succeeding in that field will not cut it. You will have to get up and make moves. The more you do this, the more clarity you will receive. It is completely okay to get involved in a field and change your mind because you discovered that it was not what you expected. That is a great thing. You have found what you don't like. That narrows your choices even more. Also, you have the courage not fall in the trap like most people do and get stuck in a job they don't like. The bottom line is you must put some skin in the game of self-discovery and that skin, at this stage of the game, is your time and energy.

Exercise F2.4 – Narrow Your Dream Job Options

The US Department of Labor has conveniently put all careers into 16 clusters. Look at the following and circle your top three.

1. Agriculture, Food & Natural Resources
2. Architecture & Construction
3. Arts, A/V Technology & Communications
4. Business Management & Administration
5. Education & Training
6. Finance
7. Government & Public Administration
8. Health Science
9. Hospitality & Tourism
10. Human Services
11. Information Technology
12. Law, Public Safety, Corrections & Security
13. Manufacturing
14. Marketing
15. Science, Technology, Engineering & Mathematics
16. Transportation, Distribution & Logistics

Using a search engine, explore the career options within each field you have chosen. Simply put, for example, "Marketing job descriptions" into a search engine and you will find quite a few resources. As you look through the jobs within each field, make a note of the ones that excite you. Now, put the names of those jobs into a search engine and read more about the duties, responsibilities, and requirements of each one.

Consider yourself done with this exercise when you have identified 3-5 jobs that excite you. Time for some exploration.

The key to doing this exercise is to identify something concrete that you can go after. Having a goal directs your day-to-day activities toward what you want. You're developing the life you desire by getting to know the career you want. Learn more about your prospective field by conducting research in the following areas:

1. **History, Theories, Current Events, & Best Practices –** Each industry has *periodicals*, *books*, and *news* outlets that keep everyone up-to-date about the industry. Identify and peruse them. If what they are talking about does not interest you, then either look deeper into a specific niche of that field or select a completely different career cluster.

2. **Associations & Organizations –** Every industry has *networks* of people who discuss the latest ideas, share information, and help each other to become better. These networks build organizations that host *events* and *conferences* to bring people together. They are key. Usually, the stars or "Who's Who" of an industry are the leaders of those organizations.

3. **Who's Who –**This is akin to slipping into the VIP section at a club. Identifying the key players in an industry will help you understand the field; moreover, you may find someone that is doing what you want to do. If so, you must

talk to them and find out how they got to where they are. Use them as a model. People love talking about themselves.

For example, let's say you wanted to be a mechanical engineer. You would search to identify the above, then pick up a copy of the *Mechanical Engineering Magazine*. You can subscribe to the *ScienceDaily* mechanical engineering newsfeed, pick up the book *The Design of Everyday Things* by Donald Norman and follow the American Society of Mechanical Engineers or the National Society of Black Engineers to learn about people like Dr. Calvin Mackie who, among other accomplishments, served on board of the Louisiana Recovery Authority, the agency that led the city of New Orleans in rebuilding efforts after Hurricanes Katrina and Rita.

Exercise F2.5 – Research Your Industry

Start with a simple online search. For example, if you are interested in medicine, start under the broad spectrum of medicine and then put the name of your field in the search engine alongside the key words italicized in the list above above: "books on medicine", "medical associations," "medical news," or "medical conferences." Read their information. Note the names of the authors of the articles and books, the staff of the associations and organizations, the people who developed the theories. These are the Who's Who. Immersing yourself by reading and talking to people in your industry will give you great awareness about the field. <u>Also, any words or abbreviations you do not know, look them up and find out what they mean.</u> Keep a log of all this information to review before you speak to someone to emphasize that you did your research. Professionals will be able to tell by the quality of the conversation if you have done your research. Do not waste anyone's time by asking questions you could have easily found on your own.

Do the same for your dream job options.

After learning about the field, find a few local people who are in the industry and ask them about it. You can find them by contacting the staff of the associations, organizations, and businesses you identified. Use your local phonebook or yellow pages. Stop by and ask people if they would take a few moments to help you learn more about the industry. If you do not have any local organizations or businesses, then call them. Here is a script you can use and some questions you can ask:

Hi my name is ______________________. How are you? I am interested in _________________ and would like to speak to ___________________________ to learn more about the field.

When you arrange a time to speak with the person, tell them a little about yourself and why you are interested in the area. Ask them questions. Here are some you can use:

1. How did you get into the field?

2. What do you like and dislike about it?

3. What do you wish you would have known when you started?

4. What should I do to become a __________________?

5. What are the best books/periodicals I should read?

6. What are the associations and organizations I should get involved in?

7. Who are the top people in the industry?

8. Ask any questions that come to your mind as you were doing your research (no matter how "stupid" you may think they are).

Through this process, not only will you be learning about the field, you will be creating relationships that may lead to job and scholarship opportunities. Start the process with people you know or who are at the bottom of the businesses and organizations. Depending on your personality, the first few times will be very intimidating but, as with all things, the more you do it, the more comfortable you will become - and the better you will get at it.

Once you become more skilled in having conversations with strangers about their work, it will be time to contact people in positions of authority. That way, they become familiar with you and impressed with your level of knowledge and interest. This alone can get you acquainted with authorities and you want to take advantage of those opportunities.

Continue this process for the rest of your life as you figure out what you want to do professionally. It is a very powerful way to build your network and knowledge about your potential vocation and/or career. This is probably the most important exercise of this book outside of discovering your field of interest. If you do this one thing very well and learn from the people in your industry, you will have all you need to succeed.

Identify the Four Pillars of Your Dream Job

You've focused on a field. You've contacted major players in the industry and are cultivating relationships with them. Money will present itself through internships, scholarships, and jobs relating to that field and weed out the petty hustles that you may have been entertaining. In truth, such blessings were in existence all along. The difference is that now your vision is focused and the lane you now move in brings them in sight.

The Four Pillars of *The Academic Hustle* are based on the qualities every job, scholarship, and internship application takes into consideration. As you create the steps to get to that high position, you will go through these four categories:

1. **Education –** What do you know? What are the degrees and certifications you have? What have you been trained in? Who trained you?

2. **Experience –** What have you done? What jobs have you held? What were your responsibilities? How well did you perform? How much experience do you have?

3. **Relationships –** What do people say about you? Who knows you? Who is recommending you? How strongly are they recommending you?

4. **Presentation –** What do you say about yourself? How well do you present yourself as the ideal candidate? Are you able to communicate in the industry's language?

Every career has these requirements. You must have the right education, experience, relationships, and present yourself in the right way to get the job you want. If you want to become anything, find out who the molds are—people who have succeeded in meeting these requirements—and form a plan to get there. The fastest and easiest way to find the right molds for what you want to do is to research 2–3 people in your dream job and identify what they did.

For example, say you want to be an astrophysicist on the level of Neil deGrasse Tyson, one of the most prominent astrophysicists of our time. Do your research and identify what he did in each area:

1. **Education -** What degrees and certifications did he receive? What schools did he attend? How well did he perform?

   Neil deGrasse Tyson studied astronomy obsessively from the age of nine. I underline obsessively for a reason. When you are setting yourself on the path to success,you cannot treat it like a cute hobby with some stuff you memorized off Wikipedia to impress somebody you want to get with. Tyson is the truth and his résumé proves this. He attended one of the top universities in the world, Harvard University, and obtained a bachelor of arts in physics. Neil then went to the University of Texas to get a master of arts in astronomy. Next, he studied at Columbia University to earn a master of philosophy and a doctor of philosophy degree in astrophysics. Neil didn't just get the grades; he continued to learn and further his education by participating on various commissions, conducting research, and publishing books.

2. **Experience -** What type of jobs did he have throughout his career? For how long? What volunteer activities did he

participate in? How long did he participate in them? What awards did he win?

At a very young age, Neil was involved in a wide array of activities. In high school, he was the captain of the wrestling team and editor-in-chief of the school's physical science journal. He was giving lectures on astronomy at the age of fifteen. In college, he was involved in wrestling, rowing, and dance. You may ask what does rowing some boat and rolling around with other guys in a unitard have to do with astrophysics? Clearly, he is not the type of guy to limit himself. He took advantage of whatever was in his reach. By doing so, the people he would eventually work alongside could have more in common with him because they may have had such experiences; outside interests made him more relatable. His being knowledgeable beyond stereotypical topics like rap and basketball made those who could open more doors for hi, take notice.

Neil participated in research programs with NASA and the ARCS Foundation. After college, he worked as a teacher at many of the top institutions in his field. He also served on presidential committees and won the top awards in his field. He now directs one of the top planetariums in the world and continues to appear on many panels and television shows.

3. **Relationships -** What networks did he become a part of? Who did he impress? What caliber of people did he interact with at each stage of his career? What were their roles and networks?

As Neil excelled in his educational endeavors continued to develop his experiences, he impressed quite a few people with his work and built a powerful network. Carl Sagan, one of the top astronomers of his time, personally tried to recruit Neil to Cornell University. US President George W. Bush appointed Neil to the highest commissions on astronomy. Working the pillars is what got him there.

4. **Presentation** – What is the language of the profession? What made him the ideal candidate? What characteristics, qualities, skills, and interests did he have?

    From a very young age, Tyson was a stellar student who was very involved in his field of interest, and interacted with many in his profession. The time invested in getting his education, developing experience, and building great relationships transformed him into the ideal candidate for the opportunities in his field. He learned the industry's jargon and how people in his field presented themselves. It is without question that while he excelled in school and gained in-depth experience, he also learned how to write and speak the language of his field eloquently.

You can start with an internet search because it is the most convenient, but by no means, should that be the be all and end all. You probably didn't start right out of elementary school doing it big, like Tyson. I know I didn't. Just get in the game where you are, as you are. Learn the pillar moves of that star in your dream job. Start handling your business in the same fashion until it will be impossible for them to ignore you.

Exercise F2.6 – Determine the Molds of Your Dream Job

As you begin to research your industry, you will come across people who are in positions you want to be in. These people are called **molds** and are quite useful. Take note of those molds. Create a document for each of them. Put their name at the top and headings for each of the **Four Pillars** with plenty of space under each one. Using the example above, identify what it took for them to get to where they are. Note everything you can think of within each pillar. You do not have to write it in paragraph form. Words, phrases, pictures, or whatever else reminds you of what they did should suffice.

Search online, use professional networking sites like LinkedIn to review résumés, read about the job, ask questions directly, and ask others who know the moves they made with the **Four Pillars.** You will be surprised at the information you can find through molds.

Use a Strength, Weakness, Opportunity, Threat (S.W.O.T) Analysis to Understand Where You Are

This isn't the SWAT team dressed in black called in to rescue hostages. Nah. When you do your research about your future area of expertise, you are essentially doing career planning research. The key to career planning is understanding where you are compared to where you want to be. That is the purpose of a S.W.O.T Analysis.

That's right, a S.W.O.T Analysis is a strategic planning method used to evaluate the strengths, weaknesses, opportunities, and threats to an endeavor. It has been a very useful tool in my personal development. The purpose is to determine what you do well (strengths), what you need to work on (weaknesses), what resources you have access to that can help you (opportunities) and what are the obstacles you must overcome (threats). Asking these questions in a variety of ways will provide you with a more realistic vision of what you must do to fulfill your mission.

I did a S.W.O.T Analysis during my first couple of weeks on campus. Here is what it looked like:

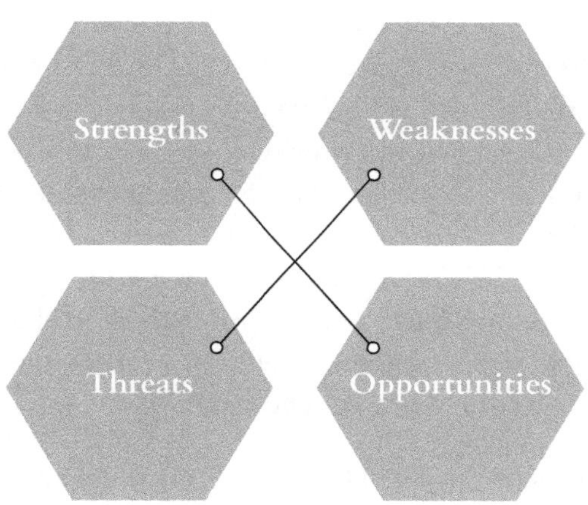

Mission: To pay for school within two years.

Strengths: I am smart. This is a game and I am good at playing games. I have a "ride or die," do whatever it takes kind of determination. I know how to read and learn on my own. I listen.

Weakness: I do not like to study. I do not know much about college life and work. I have never written a paper over three pages. I came from one of the worst schools in my district. I do not know about scholarships. I do not know how I am going to pay for school. I am scared. I am intimidated by the smart and accomplished people around me. I do not know what college is preparing me for. I do not know what to expect. I am the first in my family to do this.

Opportunities: I am in college. There are people here who have received scholarship money. There are books and other resources about scholarships all around me. I have two years to do it.

Threats: I am on academic probation. I only have two years. If I fail one class, I am kicked out. I have criminal charges and, to be honest, a bad attitude. People have a strong aversion to my hairstyle. The way I present myself makes people dismiss me because they think I am dumb and "ghetto."

This exercise took the thoughts swimming in my head and put them on paper where I could objectively figure out what I was going to do. It helped me realize that all was not lost, and that I had strengths that would give me an edge. I needed to emphasize those strengths as much as possible. My weaknesses were now on paper. It took some real maturity on my part to admit them. Many kids at that age with my background are too sensitive and "in their feelings" to be that real with themselves. Most would just blow off the S.W.O.T analysis and pout with an attitude—everything sucks too much to be worth such effort. People who can do this will save themselves a lot of heartbreak, therapy, time, and money compared to those who refuse.

I saw my threats on paper. This allowed me to step back from them and look at them objectively. I did not mistake them as irreplaceable parts of what made me who I am; but instead, as snapshots of temporary situations, states of mind, and resources at my disposal. It felt like I matured a good three years or so as a result of writing it down and studying it. My weaknesses were temporary states of being, which meant I could overcome them. They were the things I had to figure out. There were opportunities I could take advantage of to address my weaknesses. I just had to make sure I recognized and used them. Finally, I had to keep in mind the things that would hinder me. I had to figure out how I would deal with the threats to my mission.

At first, this seemed overwhelming. I did not know if I had what it took to accomplish my mission. However, I knew that did not matter. I had to do it. The WHAT and WHY of my mother, lil brother, and the rest of the family counting on me is what got me out of my bed when I tried to use the excuse of others being just as lazy. Thanks to my S.W.O.T Analysis, I could see the cards I was dealt and how best to play them in the game of life.

The S.W.O.T Analysis is a very good tool to keep you from lying to yourself. You will have no choice but to get a clear idea of where you are. Those gaps and vague areas where you're just hoping for good luck to rescue you, will jump off the page and scream at you.

Exercise F2.7 – The S.W.O.T Analysis

Block out at least 20 minutes. Create a document and put your personal mission statement at the top. Create the following headings with a lot of space under each one: *Strengths, Weaknesses, Opportunities, Threats*. Reread the section on S.W.O.T analysis. Start to fill in the space under each heading with every thought that comes to mind. Use the following questions to evaluate where you are in relation to your mission:

Strengths:

- What do you do better than people around you (friends, family, teammates, etc.)?
- What are you great at? What are your best talents or natural abilities?
- What are you most effective at? Where do you have the most impact?
- What do others say you are good at?
- What do you believe you are good at? Think professionally and personally?
- What about you will make accomplishing your mission easier?

Weaknesses:

- What do you have a harder time doing than most people around you (friends, family, teammates, etc.)?
- What do others say you need to improve on?
- What do you believe you need to improve on? Professionally and personally?
- What about you will make it harder to accomplish your mission?

Opportunities:

- Think of all the things that can help your family connections, friends, experience, insight, etc.)

Threats:

- Think of all the things that can hinder you (transportation, experience, phobias, work style, etc.)

Take time to really think through each one. The more you put on the paper the more you can use to help you develop your strategy. This is a powerful exercise worth every minute you put into it.

Define Your Steps: Goal Setting

You've written down and come to terms with your S.W.O.T Analysis. Now it is time to set up some plans and goals of how to address what S.W.O.T revealed. The importance of setting goals is essential. How many times have you heard that one? Repeatedly, I'm sure. You're about to hear it again. Goals articulate WHAT you want in measurable terms that prove to you and others that you are making progress in the right direction.

Goals are a step closer to designing the most productive day-to-day schedule one can make. Goals give you an intuitive sense of what activities lead toward achieving them and the activities that keep you from doing so. Cleaning up and fine-tuning your day-to-day routine is a major step in shaping your life. For example, having a career goal of becoming a pilot directs much of your time into doing what it takes to become a pilot instead of a hobby like sports or video games. You will know when you are not spending enough time accomplishing your goal when you are doing things that are not working toward your goal. This is not to say that you don't deserve some down time to relax, but let's be honest, you know when you could do better with how you are spending that downtime.

Set Goals for Yourself

Setting goals is simple. All it takes is WRITING down S.M.A.R.T. goals. That's right, I just hit you with another acronym. Get used to it. I can assure you that there are a quite a few acronyms waiting for you in your field of study.

S.M.A.R.T is the quality of all goals that are Specific, Measurable, Achievable, Relevant and Time-Bound. The emphasis is put on writing these types of goals down. It is amazing how resistant people are to the simple act of picking up a pen and writing a few words on paper. I notice a lot of these people are just as resistant to reading a book. It did not take me long to see that I did not want to be one of these people. Writing things down is a very powerful way to make them a reality. It helps you clearly articulate what you want in exact words.

Everyone thinks. We also have the power to turn those thoughts into reality. However, there is something about writing things down that make it that much more powerful. Maybe it is the fact that writing them down is the first concrete impression of your thoughts on this world, putting it out there into the universe in an undeniable way. Trust me on this. WRITE YOUR GOALS!

When you write your goals make them S.M.A.R.T. For example, do not just write

I want a scholarship.

Be **Specific.** Get as clear as possible. You should be able to know exactly what you want.

I need to secure $10,000 in scholarships.

Make them **Measurable.** The above is measurable because you know when you have attained it. Here is an example of something that is not measurable:

I want to work

This is bad because you can work on your house. You can work without being paid. You can work 10 years from now. How do you know when you have attained the goal? A more specific and measureable example would be:

I want to secure a job making $15 an hour within the next month.

Make sure your goal is **Achievable.** Please do not set a goal of making a million dollars by next week if you have no realistic plan of making it happen and you have not done it before. Goals need to be achievable. If not, you will only be excited to see them happen in the beginning, but doubt will grow as the days go by. Do not say I am going to become a real estate agent next week if you do not even know what a real estate agent does. Do the research to be certain of what is achievable.

Relevant. Your goals should align with your overall career plan. Double-check that. Do not have a goal to get a job as a paralegal if you want to become a doctor. Your goals need to align.

Time-Bound. If your goal does not have a date attached to it then the chance of it being accomplished, in any reasonable amount of time, is slim. Putting a timeframe to your goal creates urgency. In addition, everything happens in time. Therefore, to accomplish anything, you must put it within a timeframe.

Here is a great example of a goal for someone wanting to be an accountant:

I will pass the CPA exam by the end of the year.

If you didn't know, a CPA or Certified Public Accountant, is a financial advisor who helps businesses, individuals, and other organizations plan and reach their financial goals.

Taxes are an important part of reaching financial goals. So, after the CPA exam, a fitting time-bound goal could be:

I will start my own tax preparation business within two years.

Whatever your goals are, make sure they are S.M.A.R.T. Also, keep in mind that when life happens, goals change. That is fine. Just be sure to continuously review and update them. This process will begin to define your life, instead of you feeling like it is being blown in any which way at the mercy of the wind.

People who set goals create the lives they want to live. They become the master of their lives. Why? Because they have it set in their mind. They have written it down. They know exactly what they should and should not be doing with their time every day. They spend their time doing the things they want, which in turn, creates the life they want.

Exercise F3.1 – Goal Setting

Review Exercises 1.7 – 10. Write down 3 – 5 S.M.A.R.T. goals associated with your personal mission and/or your career.

Break Them Down into Objectives

Goals are good to have but they are not enough. Our goals can overwhelm us. They are sometimes too big and take too long to realize. As we move toward them, we may become discouraged because we are putting in the work, but it does not look like we are getting any closer to achieving it. Objectives are the cure.

Objectives help us monitor our progress. They break our goals into bite-sized targets that we can hit along the way. Goals are long-term aspirations; objectives are short-term targets. For example, my goal was to get school paid for in two years. My objectives were to:

- Get over a 3.5 GPA every semester
- Participate in a major community service project each semester
- Get on the executive board of two clubs by sophomore year
- Secure a recommendation from a teacher each semester
- Update a spreadsheet with all the details for potential scholarships each semester

As I began to meet these objectives, I felt better and better about accomplishing my goal. Moreover, it built the momentum that kept me excited and focused.

Whenever you have a goal, break it down into S.M.A.R.T. objectives. Your objectives should cover different aspects of your goal and have a much shorter deadline. When you do this, your objectives should feel like steps toward your goal. If meeting objectives become a long-term effort and require too many details, then treat them like a goal and break them down even further.

Try not to make this rocket science. Simply develop measurable, time-bound targets that will serve as guideposts toward your goals.

Exercise F3.2 – Making Objectives

Review Exercises 1.11. Write down S.M.A.R.T. objectives for your goals.

Develop Your Strategies

Having goals and objectives put you way ahead of others. However, if you have no idea how you are going to accomplish them, then they are fantasies and "ain't nobody got time" for people sitting around hoping to wish their way to something. Dr. Martin Luther King Jr. had a dream and that dream was that the world respect you based on the merits of your character and hustle. Barack Obama won the presidency with the theme of hope for a better future. You are that hope, so get to manifesting it by developing your strategies, your goals, and objectives.

Strategies are the how. How do you plan to meet your objectives? What are your methods of action?

We have been strategizing throughout this section. We have identified what we want, conducted research to figure out the components of what we want, and begun to set goals and objectives. The rest of this book details how to set yourself up in the best possible situation for each of these components. As you progress through the book, keep asking yourself, "What is the best possible way to go about this? What would make me a top candidate? What does the best look like?"

Strategizing is literally the act of knowing what you want, understanding where you are, and figuring out the best path between the two. Figuring out the best path requires trial and error, learning from others, and modifying your path based upon new insights and any changes in situations. Be prepared to bump your head a few times from trial and error. That's life; it's not some bitter truth that proves your haters were right or that you don't deserve to make it. Being dramatic about the trial and error process to success, or making more out of it than it is, is only a waste of imagination. You are tough. Prove it to yourself and the world.

If you follow your dreams, you can accomplish anything.
If you always do your best they your destiny is king of the world.

—**Dead Prez, "The Game of Life"**

Exercise F3.3 – Develop Your Strategic Plan

For this exercise we are going to put everything we covered into one document.

1. Create a document and put your personal mission statement at the top.

2. Under your personal mission statement put your dream job. If you have more than one, create a separate document for each one and put your personal mission statement at the top.

3. Create sections for each of the Four Pillars. Within each section write your goals and objectives for the pillar.

Keep this document close to you. If you have an agenda or folder for school, put it in the front. If you have it electronically, put it on your desktop. Put it on top of your phone before you go to bed to force yourself to revisit it in the morning. You should be able to remind yourself of your mission and the steps you need to accomplish it at any time.

Know this:

- Take time to identify what you want out of life and why you want it.
- Craft a personal mission statement and put it where you will be reminded of it daily.
- Your ***dream job*** is out there. Identify what it is and the ***Four Pillars*** of education, experience, relationships, and presentation to secure it.
- Do your research to develop a career plan: talk to people, read, and get to know your industry.
- Analyze yourself using a S.W.O.T analysis to identify where you are and what you need to focus on to accomplish your mission.
- Set S.M.A.R.T. goals and objectives that lead to the accomplishment of your mission.

The Four Pillars of The Academic Hustle

Understand the system, then master the game

Pillar #1: *Get the Best Education*

Education is the passport to the future, for tomorrow belongs to those who prepare for it today.

—Malcolm X

Education is transformational. You can learn and transform into mechanic, teacher, banker, social worker, astrophysicist, or even a spiritual teacher. As you read this, people in those fields are retiring and passing away. Someone must take their positions, so whatever your heart desires, you can learn it and become it.

In this section you will learn:

- The types of educational institutions and which one is best for your career goal.
- How to decide on your specialized area of study.
- Strategies for excelling in school and increasing your value with As.

As you progress in your personal transformation, your value in society increases. You have decided to put in the extra effort to learn more than others about a specific subject, so your opinion, insights, and know-how becomes valuable. People exchange their money for value. The more valuable you become, the more you will be paid.

The easiest and quickest way to increase your value is through education. Moreover, once you have it, it can never be taken away from you. I know you have heard that a million times from old folks, but it is true. No one can yank the title of master chef from someone who has earned it, ever. As you attain a certain level of education, you are awarded some type of recommendation or certification acknowledging that you can utilize what you learned. Some people out there may not like you, but they will never be able to deny what you achieved in this regard. Such a certification can take the form of a diploma, a degree, or someone or an institution affirming that you know what you know. The institution or person who trained you will be a critical factor in your career development. Pick the right institution carefully.

Select the Right Institution

Educational institutions are critical for developing three things:

1. **Education –** Providing insight into various fields and teaching you what you need to know to operate in the field of your choice.

2. **Experiences –** Exposing you to various professions and providing opportunities for you to work, volunteer, and/or experience your career field.

3. **Relationships –** Creating an environment where you can connect with people (professors, students, professionals, etc.) who will empower your life and career.

Most people focus solely on their majors and the diploma. Bad move. That's very short-sighted. Classes are the foundation of the academic environment; however, it is only one aspect of what an educational institution has to offer. When selecting an institution, you want to take into consideration a wide range of factors.

Most people select institutions based on the ones their family and friends suggest or what they see in their environment. It's understandable—that is human nature. To ensure you get the best return on your investment of so much time and money, please look at the return they have given to other people who have attended. Focus on their product, their graduates, and the people they produce. Do some serious research on their alumni and ask yourself:

- What is the reputation of the graduates?
- What are the graduates doing?
- How have their graduates affected change in the world?
- Are these graduates making the types of salaries that I'm aiming for?

Knowing about the alumni gives you an idea of what the institution's value is in the world and what type of network you will be in. The results they tend to produce are the most likely scenario for what you will do. What type of jobs are their graduates being offered? Are they in your field? Where are they located? Are they in the high-end, middle, or low-end of the job market? Do they give back to their community? Do they do the things you care about? Are they in the positions you want to be in? Are they the type of people you want to associate with? These are very important questions to answer. Make a point to find these answers before you commit. Just going somewhere to get a degree screams desperation and poor planning. Selecting the right institution is a bigger decision than buying a house or car. This is a lifelong community you're considering aligning yourself with, just like marrying into a family.

Most institutions fall into the following categories:

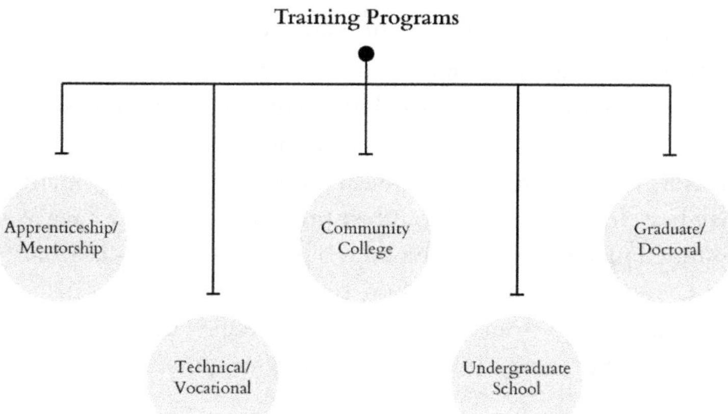

Apprenticeships/Mentorship

Apprenticeships are the most common form of specialized education in the world. They have been used for thousands of years to pass down traditions, insights, and expertise. Most people will receive this type of education at some point in their lives. While there are many formal apprenticeship programs, this type of education usually takes the form of a mentorship. Apprenticeships are formal mentorships where someone more experienced than you will help to guide your development in a specific area.

If you know exactly what you want to do in life, this is the best way to get there fast. A mentor can guide you through the best trainings for you, the best experience-building activities, connect you with the right people, and ensure your development into the ideal candidate. The key to getting the most out of this type of training is to pick the right person.

First, your mentor should be doing what you want to do. Second, they must be willing to guide you. As you research your industry (Exercise 2.5), you will come across quite a few people. Be on the lookout for those who fulfill the two requirements above. When you identify potential mentors, latch on to them and develop a great relationship (Pillar #3) with them. If the relationship develops well, you will have yourself a mentor.

One point to keep in mind about mentors: do not believe they know everything about everything. A mentor guides your development in a specific area. They may guide you in more than one area; however, it would be ideal to have multiple mentors for each area of your life and career. Your career mentor may have focused so much on their profession that they have a dysfunctional personal life. Nobody's perfect, but you get what I'm saying. Learn the tricks of the trade about being a great physical therapist from a great physical therapist. Learn how to be great parent or spouse from a great parent or spouse.

Apply this understanding of mentorship to any apprenticeship programs of your choosing. You want to make sure that the apprenticeship program will prepare you for what you want to do. You should get the certifications and licenses you need and feel comfortable that the on-the-job training you receive is preparing you for what you want.

Technical/Vocational/Career School

Technical/vocational schools are usually two-year programs that prepare you for a specific trade. As with apprenticeship programs, these are perfect for someone who knows what they want to do. A technical program gives you the skills and certifications you need to enter directly into your specific field.

Selecting a technical school is all about the connections your institution has with the market you are entering. Technical schools provide standard certifications. You want to make sure that those certifications are recognized in your industry. If the school is known in your market and has connections with local businesses, then it should be a good choice. Be sure to take the time to explore the institution and, more importantly, your instructor's relationship with local businesses. Employers recruit from schools.

Community/Junior College

Community colleges are valuable resources in their communities. They can offer certifications, diplomas, associate degrees, and continuing/adult education classes at reasonable prices. Community colleges can be great for those who know what they want to do because they may have the program that will give you exactly what you need. It is also a great place for those that do not know what they want to do because it can be used as a cost-effective stepping-stone to get into another school.

If you have a specific program in mind, make sure the certificate you receive is respected in your industry. If you are using a community college as a stepping-stone to get into another school, check with the school(s) you will be transferring to, to ensure that your credits will be accepted. There is nothing more frustrating than attending a school only to find that your credits are not transferable, which means you have wasted your time and money. For those who are unsure of what they want to do, take a few classes in your area of interest without enrolling in a program to test it out. Community colleges can also be great resources for continuing professional development and exploring career possibilities.

Undergraduate School

Undergraduate school is what most people refer to when they talk about college. When people advocate going to college, they are usually emphasizing getting at least a bachelor of arts or sciences degree. However, the most important aspects of undergraduate school are not the degree you receive, but the experiences you have and the relationships you build.

Words cannot explain the innumerable amount of life-changing experiences a respectable and supportive undergraduate environment can create. Studying abroad, leading organizations of people, conducting research, meeting industry leaders, organizing events, late-night debates/arguments/conversations (whatever you want to call them), and partying are just a few of the amazing experiences the right undergraduate institution can provide for you. The undergrad experience is unlike anything you will ever have in your life.

College changed my life. Most people who went away to college or lived on campus will say the same thing. That is why I strongly suggest that if you want to have the best experience possible, read these words carefully: GO AWAY TO COLLEGE and IMMERSE YOURSELF IN THE UNDERGRADUATE EXPERIENCE! Getting away from home, family, and friends creates an environment for your personality to blossom. Such an experience is like being in an adult incubator. Living on campus ensures you have access to everything that environment has to offer. It forces you to grow in ways that driving back to momma's across town from campus will never provide. You find ways to make do and survive which will make you proud every time you look back on it. You experiment, grow, and change without fear of the old neighborhood popping up and stressing you about your new hairstyle, philosophy, or clothes. You find out who you are in the purest sense. If you pick the right institution, have a good idea of what you want to do, and attend college right out of high school. It can be one of the most fruitful times of your life.

I am jealous of you, reader. I wish I had this book when I was just starting to take my grind seriously. I totally lucked up with Morehouse College being the right school for me. I only applied because my mother bugged me to no end about applying. What it could mean for me only became apparent when many of the men I respected were not only excited about me going but went out of their way to get me there.

When choosing the right institution, go online, talk to people who attend or work at the college, and visit the school yourself. **Do your due diligence.** Just glancing at the attractive pictures on a school's website can throw you off big time. You would not buy a house or car without thinking about it, researching it, and making sure it was what you wanted, for the price you can afford. The same logic applies to choosing a school.

Graduate/Doctoral School

For graduate school, your college choice should primarily be based upon the faculty and the degree's level of respect in your industry. For example, if you want to work on Wall Street, then getting an MBA from Wharton School at the University of Pennsylvania will open a lot more doors than getting one from an online institution. Alternatively, if you plan to work in a specific geographic region, then getting an MBA from the most respected school in that area would probably be on par, if not better, then going to a top institution out of state. This is primarily because of the relationships that school has with the local community and the number of opportunities that will afford you while you are in school. Another example: if you want to be a professor at an Ivy

League institution, then getting a PhD from another Ivy League institution will gain you a lot more respect.

To pick the best graduate school for you, be clear on what you want to do and where you want to work. Unlike undergrad, what you do in graduate school is more specifically directed toward what you will do professionally. Next, you must be laser-focused on the specific department you are considering. You want to make sure that you select a program that can prepare you for your career goal, put you in the best position to achieve it, and attain connections in the industry of your choice.

****Special note about doctoral programs**** The faculty is everything. When selecting a doctoral program, research the faculty thoroughly. Make sure you have a *few* that align with your research interests. You will be in a tough situation if you pick an institution because of one professor and that professor leaves. Your professors are the gatekeepers. At least three to five will make up your dissertation committee and they will decide if you become a PhD. It is very political. Being able to develop great relationships with your professors can make the process dramatically smooth.

Special Notes

HBCUs

I am a huge advocate of Historically Black Colleges and universities for Black people. These institutions were created for Black people when they were not allowed to attend any other schools. As a result, their purpose is to educate and develop Black people. No other group can tell you about your culture, your place in the world, and the best way to navigate it better than your own. Taking the time to experience this unique environment in America can be life-changing. There's a different atmosphere and culture within these universities, especially during the undergraduate experience, which empowers people of color more than any other institution. Check them out.

For-profit

For-profit institutions serve a community in ways that traditional institutions often ignore. As with all colleges, you want to make sure you do your research. Visit the school, talk to the students, and evaluate their graduates. Some of these colleges are not accredited. Which means, the coursework you complete during your time there will not be recognized by other schools. Make sure that your investment will be worth it. You are a customer—make you sure you're getting what you ordered.

Exercise P1.1 – Selecting the Right Institution

Unless you are going school as an undergrad with a goal of going to graduate school, your primary reason for selecting an institution should be based on your career goals.

1. Review Exercise F2.6. Take note of how the people who are in your dream job were educated. What degrees or certifications did they receive? What type of institutions awarded heir certifications? How is that institution ranked in the field?
2. Identify similar institutions. Look at the best schools in your industry without concern for geography. Then select institutions in the geographic area where you want to attend school and/or work.
3. Research those institutions by exploring their website, asking people about the school, and by calling and visiting them. Try and answer as many of these questions as possible:

    - **Education –** What type of education do they offer? Technical or liberal arts? What majors and minors do they have? What will you learn? How is the program you are interested in ranked in the field? What is the quality of the teachers?

- **Experiences –** What type of activities do they have outside of class? How much practical experience do they offer? How often do they bring people, organizations, and businesses into the training environment? What is the caliber of people that come to the institution? What are the travel and student exchange opportunities? What are the things to do outside of and around the institution? What extracurricular activities can you get involved with while there? Do they have partnerships with businesses?

- **Relationships –** How well-connected are your teachers? Do the student demographics reflect the people you would like to be around? What is the student-teacher ratio? What types of people attend? Are the students as awesome as you want to be? How helpful are the teachers and staff? How is the alumni network? How much time do the teachers spend with students outside of class?

4. Rank the institutions based upon how well they meet your preferred answers to the questions above. Then put them into the following categories:

   - **Challenge -** the ones that you may not get into
   - **Reach –** ones that may be a challenge to attend
   - **Sure –** institutions you know you will get into

5. Narrow your list to no more than 10 institutions. You want to be able to tailor your application to each of them (we will talk more about this in Pillar #4).

For those going to undergrad with an expectation of attending graduate school, select your institution based upon the experiences and relationships. The undergraduate experience can be an extremely fun and rewarding one in and of itself. The graduate school you attend will be the primary qualification your next opportunity will use to evaluate you and your educational background. Pick an undergraduate institution you will enjoy and a graduate school that will set you up for your career.

Decide on Your Area of Study

As with everything in this book, your course of study should be based upon your career goals. Being as clear as possible on those goals will ensure you choose the best course of study. If you have not selected a career path, continue to review and complete the exercises in F2 before deciding upon an area of study, unless it is in an undergraduate program.

For those going to an undergraduate school, if you do not know what you want to do in life, picking a major can help you start to narrow your choices. Take time and make your selection carefully. Many institutions do not require you to select a major until your sophomore year. That can work for you, because in the meantime, you take required courses that you would have to take regardless of your major. And while changing majors is understandable, most people do so because they have not taken the time to really consider what they want to do. Instead, they let their academic advisors, parents, friends, or the job market dictate their course of study.

I went to a small liberal arts college as a business administration major. I chose this course of study because my mother and many of my mentors were in business. In addition, I wanted to make money. As I began attending classes, I became curious about what other courses the schoo had to offer, so much that I took the course catalog to my room and on an afternoon when I did not have much planned, I did the following:

1. Skimmed over all the course offerings and noted the names of any that sounded somewhat interesting.

2. Next, I looked through all the classes in each major I chose and noted the classes in that major that were somewhat interesting. (If you select more majors during the first step than you would like to go through, conduct a process of elimination and start to compare your majors with each other and remove the ones that are less interesting until you get to the number of majors you are comfortable looking through.)

3. Upon completing the first two steps, I had a document that had all the majors I was interested in and their classes. There were four majors that had the majority of classes: African American studies, psychology, sociology, and philosophy.

4. I visited each department, talked to the teachers and students, took a few classes, and researched potential career opportunities.

5. After that process, I decided to major in my top two and had plans to minor in the others. (You could either pick the major that has the most classes, use the process of elimination in step two to select your major from your top choices, or select a couple of the top majors and do some more research.)

Take the amount of time necessary to make your choice. Remember, this is your single most important decision. You would be amazed at the time and tens of thousands of dollars people waste because they have changed majors or wasted time taking classes they did not need. Additionally, it is common for someone to work in a career after college that has nothing to do with their degree.

Exercise P1.2 – Deciding on Your Course of Study

Once you have selected an institution, review your notes from the exercises in F2. Peruse the course catalog of your institution and use the example above to select a course of study.

Pick Your Classes Strategically

The primary reason we go to school is to take classes. Classes are the place where teachers share their knowledge and where students absorb it. Teachers give assignments and tests to assess how well their students have learned the information they are imparting. *The Academic Hustle* looks at classes in two ways:

1. As a means to learn and grow

2. As a means to look better

A lot of people aren't up on the level of appreciating number two. If you are taking a class to learn about a subject that you are interested in, and to grow your knowledge in that area, then you will be a more engaged student. You will want to show up to class more regularly. If you look at class to make your transcript look better, then you will do what you must do to get that 'A'. Look at your transcript as another facet of your résumé.

The Academic Hustle does not look at classes as a means to get a degree. Those who do that focus on just passing. That mentality breeds uninspired, mediocre, or poor students. Moreover, the skills, intelligence, and work ethic gained by people who get As are attractive to companies.

Classes are a significant aspect of school, and they are your opportunity to learn what you need to prepare yourself for the next step. Do not just focus on the subject of a particular class.

We all have taken classes that seem not to apply directly to what we want to do; however, they may challenge your mind to think, read, and write in a certain way. The more ways you are challenged, the more you will grow.

As mentioned, everything we talk about focuses on setting yourself up for the next step. Getting As in all your classes will make you a very competitive candidate for your future goals (and get you paid with scholarships).

If you wanted to get a PhD in astronomy, the selection committee will be evaluating how well you performed in math and physics classes. If you only took a few and performed poorly in them, then you most likely will not be a competitive candidate. If you wanted to go to law school, they are going to look at the rigor of the classes you took, especially those that involved critical thinking and writing. Therefore, you must be strategic about what classes you take and ensure that those classes set you up for your next step. This is not the place to try and get by with excuses and below average work, and thinking people who like you or feel sorry for you will make up for it. Life will definitely show you better than it can tell you.

Pick your classes for three reasons:

1. **Fulfill Requirements:** All degrees, diplomas, certifications, majors, or minors have basic requirements. Find out what classes are required and be sure to take them. It is your responsibility, not your academic advisor's responsibility, to know what classes these are and make sure you take them. Some may only be there for the paycheck and will put in anything just to get you out of their faces, so if your major is biology and you're in some basket weaving class you're not the least bit into, it's on you. Some classes are only offered certain semesters, so it is important to plan ahead and register early.

2. **Set Yourself Up for The Next Level:** Make sure that every class you take is preparing you for what you want to

do in the future. Your focus needs to be on taking classes you know will be attractive to the selection committee for your next step and picking teachers who will write strong recommendations to help you get to that next step—or challenge you to become better.

3. **What You Enjoy:** There are sometimes lists of classes you can choose from to fulfill the requirements of your degree. Evaluate the options and pick the ones that are the most interesting and appealing to you. If you do not know what you want to do, these options give you the opportunity to be exposed to new ideas that may help you figure that out.

If you choose classes with information you are interested in, the likelihood of doing well in that class will increase exponentially. I am a strong advocate of doing what you love. Here's why:

1. When you do what you enjoy or love, you will be much better at it which translates into earning more As.

2. Your teachers and peers will recognize your level of engagement. People share opportunities with people who they believe are interested in them and will take advantage of the opportunity.

3. The money will come, or it will not matter. When you do what you love, you tend to be better at it. As a result, people will pay you more. And "if" you become "stuck" in something you enjoy, you'll still be happy.

Now that you know what classes you want to take, here are tips on how to best set them up:

1. **Pick Based Upon Your Schedule** – You have a choice. Choose to go to class when it works for you. If you are a late-night person, do not pick morning classes. When you go to class tired, frustrated, or lazy, your teacher will notice. Set yourself up to be engaged while you are there.

2. **Have Gaps** – Try not to take classes back-to-back. Sometimes, I believe there is a conspiracy among teachers - they like to schedule tests and set big deadlines on the same day. Having a gap (30 – 60 minutes) in between classes will give you the time you need to prepare for each class.

3. **Pick Challenging Teachers** – Relationships are your net worth. Excelling in the department chair's class can provide you with a strong recommendation option. In addition, teachers who challenge their students stretch their minds and prepare them for the real world. If you can get through a few challenging teachers with As, you will undoubtedly stand out among your peers.

Pick your classes strategically and you will set yourself up to excel.

Exercise P1.3 – Cheat Code to Picking Classes Strategically

Make a habit of registering for classes as early as possible. At least a month before registration for classes opens, begin this process:

1. Review your graduation requirements. Write down all the classes you can take during the upcoming semester.

2. Review the classes you have an option of taking. Usually, institutions will require you to take a certain amount of optional classeas that fall under certain categories of study that are sometimes unrelated to your major. Sometimes these are referred to as electives. Write down classes based upon those that will set you up for your future goals and your interests.

3. When these lists are created, use the time up until registration to identify the best teachers.

4. On the first night of registration, pick the best teachers and classes that fit your schedule for that semester. Keep in mind that requirements take priority. Earn As.

Earn 'A's

Scholarships, colleges, jobs, and others evaluate whether you are a good candidate by how you have performed in previous situations. As a student, your primary performance is based upon how well you do in each class. To make it simple, schools have designed a letter-based grading system to communicate to everyone your performance in a specific class. To determine how well you performed in a certain area (major, semester, year, etc.), they have assigned points to each of those letters. The letter grades are added up and averaged to give you your GPA.

For most schools in the USA[3], the breakdown of those letter grades and the amount of points given to each one is as follows:

A = 4

B = 3

C = 2

D = 1

F = 0

The GPA is calculated[4] by taking the sum of your grades and dividing them by the number of grades added up. For example, if

3 This is based on the standard grading system used by most schools in the USA. However, all grading systems have a way to tell if someone has failed to meet the requirements, passed, and passed with high marks. Read through this example and apply this understanding to the grading system of your institution. The primary point is to strive for the highest marks.

4 When you receive credit hours for a class, you calculate your **cumulative GPA** by 1) multiplying the numerical value of your grade by the number of credits you receive from each class. This provides the number of quality points for that class. 2) Add the total quality points for each class then divide that number by the total number of credit hours you took. The result is your cumulative GPA.

you get an A, B, C, D, and F, then your GPA will be calculated as follows,

$$4 + 3 + 2 + 1 + 0 = 10 / 5 = 2.0 \text{ GPA}$$

If you get an A, A, B, D, F, F, C, and B, then your GPA will be calculated like this,

$4 + 4 + 3 + 1 + 0 + 0 + 2 + 3 = 17 / 8 = 2.13$ GPA

It is very important to know your GPA. It is the measuring tool that people use to understand how well you performed in school.

These letter grades and numbers have a meaning. While there is not a standard definition for each letter grade, we have a general idea of what they are telling us:

F = Fail

D = Fail

C = Pass

B = Okay

A = Awesome

For most institutions, you need at least a 2.0 to graduate, which means that anything below a 2.0 is failure. A C means you did just enough to pass. Cs are NOT good grades. Just passing, just qualifying, making it just in time is not a good sign to anyone. You are basically the "Cream of the Crap," which means you still stink. Institutions and companies want people who are above "just getting by."

Therefore, any GPA that starts with a 2 is mediocre. A 2 is associated with a C and means you did just enough to get by… you barely made it. A C average will be accepted by some companies in the job market, but you will most likely be offered positions and salaries as unappealing as your grades.

I was ill equipped to get As when I got to college. To my credit, I read quite a few books on how to excel in school. The best two were *Excellence Without Excuse: The Black Student's Guide to Academic Excellence* by Charles Cherry and *Tricks of the Grade* by Dr. Joe Martin. During my first semester in college, the lessons I learned in those books helped me earn a GPA over 3.5.

This is the grading scale Dr. Martin recommends you keep mind:

A = Great

B = Okay

F = Failure

Remember, okay is not acceptable! The only grade you should be satisfied with is an A. Here is why:

First, when applying for anything or telling someone your grade, there is an unspoken understanding of what your GPA is saying. We already know that anything below a 2.0 is considered failure, and anything that begins with a 2 is average so the rest breaks down as follows:

3.7 – 4.0 – You are an awesome student, an academic beast! You are among the best of the best. There is no doubt about your intelligence. This GPA will seal the deal with almost any scholarship. You will be one of the top candidates.

3.5 – 3.7 – You are a very smart student. This GPA will make you very competitive for many scholarships.

3.3 – 3.5 – You are a smart student. This GPA will also make you competitive for some scholarships.

3.0 – 3.3 – You did well in school. You made it into the game for scholarships. However, you are at the bottom.

So as you can see, the higher your GPA, the more competitive you are for scholarships and the better prospect you are after graduation.

With this in mind, the second reason you should always strive for an A is that it is the only grade that can get you above a 3.0. Earning straight Bs will get you a 3.0. The more As you get the higher your GPA. Think about every A you get as money in the bank. In addition, when you submit an application, you are basically filling out a withdrawal slip to get your money.

The more you fill your transcript with As, the better. In addition, if those As are in more challenging classes like honors, Advance Placement, or International Baccalaureate, even better. However, *do not fool yourself into thinking that a B in a harder class is equal to an A in a lower class.* Technically, you are right if you think about how the grade is "weighed." However, it still means you are average in that class. And, if you get a C in a harder class, it still means that you just passed. **Focus on making sure your *unweighted GPA* is as high as possible and let the rest take care of its self.**

Finally, the most important reason to always strive for an A: life happens. Think about it. If you are aiming just to pass a class and something randomly bad comes up or you slip up (fail a test, miss an assignment, get a bad grade on a major project, etc.), what do you think will happen? You will fail. Failure is not an option; therefore, it is never good to just try to pass a class.

Now if you strive for a B and you slip up, more than likely you will earn a C. However, if something really bad happens (death in the family, long sickness, loss all your work, etc.) or you slip up seriously, then you will most likely fail.

On the other hand, always striving for an A is the mentality of someone who believes failure is not an option.

The point is that if you always do what it takes to get an A you will, at the very least, pass the class. At best, you will be among the best of the best and be the most competitive person for all types of scholarships, fellowships, programs, and awards.

If you are failing classes, not only are you wasting your own time and money, you are also at risk of losing future funding for school. The federal government has something called Satisfactory Academic Progress (SAP). If you do not pass enough classes, they will take away your federal funding. Consistently failing classes is idiotic. Don't be idiotic.

It is not impossible for us to get an A and we know it. I speak to quite a few students and 98 percent of the time when I ask them if getting an A is too hard or impossible, they say it is not. When I did my research on high-academic achievers, the most important factor for earning an A was time management. There was nothing new, extravagant or special that they did. Getting an A is all about how much time you put into the class.

For those who say getting an 'A' is too hard ask yourself these questions:

1. Do you show up for class on time at least 90 percent of the time?

2. Do you pay attention and take notes?

3. Do you do all your homework?

4. Do you study for each class outside of class?

5. Do you write more than one draft of your essays?

6. Do you regularly ask for assistance from your teacher, teacher's assistant, tutor, or other 'A' students?

If you did not say yes immediately to each of these questions, then you are fooling yourself into thinking it is "too hard" to get an A. These are the basics to being a good student.

Do the Basics

Most people think getting an 'A' is hard work. Sometimes it is. But, many times taking care of the basics is all you need to do.

1. **Show up to class** – The whole point of enrolling in school is to take classes to learn what you need for your career. Every class missed is a missed training opportunity. Plus, teachers prepare lesson plans and lecture notes to ensure they cover what you need to know for tests and assignments. The more you know of what they want you to know, the better shot you have at getting an A.

2. **Take notes** – Professionals write things down. They need to create logs of what was said or what needs to be done so they can always refer to it, if needed. Developing that habit in school will not only set you up for making As, it will prepare you for the working world.

3. **Read the book** – Most of what you need to know for a class is in the books that are assigned. Do not hold yourself back by not reviewing that material. Underline, highlight, and take notes so that you can make sense of what you need to know to get an A.

4. **Do the work –** Assignments are study materials. They train you in what you need to know and give you the opportunity to practice making As. Every opportunity you can get to get an A needs to be taken advantage of.

5. **Study –** Reading the book and doing the work is studying. For some people, that is all they need to prepare themselves to get As. I was a lot slower than most people. I needed much more time with the material to understand it. If you are not getting As, spend even more time studying and apply various study skills. Look online to learn about study skills or pick up the book *Excellence Without Excuse: The Black Student's Guide to Academic Excellence* by Charles Cherry.

I am constantly shocked at the number of students who go to school and do not do these things. These are the basics of being a student. Basketball players must exercise, practice, and study their opponents. Those are the basics of being a basketball player. If you are a student who is struggling to make an A, all you need to do is strengthen these basics.

Get the Teacher on Your Side

Your teachers are the most important factor in earning an A. Think about it. Your teachers develop the curriculum for the class. They tell you what to read, decide what material to discuss during class, give the assignments, AND then grade them. Simply put, they are your gatekeepers. They are the most important influence on your grade outside of you. And guess what? They are human just like you, your family and friends.

Just like you and every other human being, teachers have a bias toward the people they like and dislike. Like most of us, teachers like people who like what they like. Most of the time, teachers either enjoy being a teacher and/or the course they are teaching. Therefore, the more interest you show in the class and the more engaged you are, the more teachers are going to like you. And when they like you, they help you out. Therefore, you want to make a good impression on them.

First impressions count. On the first day of class, dress professionally. Do not go to class on the first day in pajamas or as if you are going out to a club. Never go to class in anything less than business casual. School is a professional environment. Dressing professionally will make a strong impression on your teachers. Just because a bunch of students (and maybe even some teachers) don't care enough to put on proper clothes, doesn't mean it isn't a professional environment. Teachers wear business casual clothes because they are working. So if you want to be respectful of their work, act in a professional manner as well.

Another thing you can do to create an impression on your teachers is to talk to them. Go to them during their office hours and engage with them after class. There's a trick I got from Dr. Joe Martin's book *Tricks of the Grade* that set the tone for my relationships with teachers: I would ask every one of them five questions as soon as I had the chance to pull them aside. Usually, this was immediately after the first day of class or during their office hours:

1. How long have you been teaching this class?
2. Why this subject?
3. How can I get the most out of your class?
4. What does it take to get an 'A' in this class?
5. What should I concentrate on to get an 'A' in your class?

Asking these questions should give you great insight into how to get an A in the class. The first two establishes your interest in the teacher. Most teachers teach the courses they teach because they prefer giving lessons on that subject above anything else. A teacher that is passionate about a subject will appreciate a student who engages him or her on the topic. The next three questions let the teacher know that you are serious about the class and want to get the most out of it. Usually, during questions three and four, teachers will give general answers, however, with the last question you should take notes. You need to write down everything they say and make it a point to DO IT.

Another thing to keep in mind is that teachers have eyes: they take note of the student who comes in late, sits in the back of the class, plays on their phone and does not pay attention. Some of you may say, "There is over a hundred students in my class, my teacher doesn't notice me." However, they DO notice the engaged students. You can't make a good impression on someone who does not even know you exist in this world. Therefore, you need to be an engaged student to make a good impression on a teacher. Here are what teachers like to see:

- Arrive on time or early.
- Be attentive and take notes.
- Sit in the front of the class.
- Engage with teachers about discussion topics and ask thoughtful questions.

You will be amazed at how teachers will gravitate toward engaged students. Engaged students make a teacher's job worth doing and everyone likes to feel that what they are doing something meaningful.

It makes no sense to show up, go to the back of the class, and not pay attention. What are you in school for? Doing that puts up a big sign to the teacher saying, "I don't care about this class, you, or whatever you have to say. You are not even worth my attention." How would you react to a person that does not pay attention to you? Would you help them out? If they came to you with their problems asking for a break would you give it to them? On the other hand, if you were a teacher and there was a student that did almost all the things you like to see, what would you do in those situations?

I made such an impression on my teachers that I was able to get homework assignments deadlines extended and tests delayed. Think about it. If your best student is having problems taking in all the information, where do you think the other students are? Teachers don't want to see their students fail, so when they can, they will extend or delay for the benefit of the class. Get the teacher on your side so you can put yourself in the best position to get those As.

Keep Yourself Organized

When I conducted my research on students who had a cumulative GPA of 3.3 or higher, the top two strategies for getting As were personal organization and time management. We will talk more about time management later, but for now, be sure to do the following:

1. **Have a folder for each class –** One in which you have paper for notes, a pocket for handouts, and one for completed work. All your information for class should be in one place. You should be able to identify exactly where something should be whenever you need it.

2. **Have an agenda –** A simple weekly agenda that has space under each day to list homework assignments, tests, and due dates should suffice. Once you get an agenda, USE IT!

These two items should be with you at every class. When you receive any paperwork, it should go in its proper place in the class folder. Also, if there are any due dates on the board, syllabus, or mentioned in class, it should be written immediately on the designated day in your agenda.

Exercise P1.4 – Setting Yourself Up to Earn 'A's

At the beginning of each semester go through the following process:

1. Calculate your cumulative GPA. Then set a GPA goal for the current semester (hint…it should be a 4.0).

2. Create a folder for each of your classes. On the front of the folder or immediately inside, write reminders to do any of the basics you are struggling to maintain. Bring that folder to every class and review it right before class starts.

3. Get the teacher on your side. Ask the questions noted above as soon as possible. Write the answers down in the folder for that class. Do those things and make it a point to do all the things teachers like to see throughout the course.

4. Stay organized. Keep your folder organized and agenda up-to-date.

5. Read the two books I recommended.

While the title of this book is *The Academic Hustle,* you may have noticed that it doesn't focus too much on academics. When people say, "Grades aren't everything" they are speaking the truth. However, that does not mean grades are not important. They are VERY important. Your educational background is one of the **Four Pillars** colleges, scholarships, internships, fellowships, and jobs will evaluate you on. Make it a point to be as awesome as possible in this area.

Keep these in mind:

- Strategically select the training institution that will prepare you for your career and give you the best experiences for your life. The institution you choose will be one of the most important decisions you make.
- Being clear on your area of study before committing to one will save you a lot of money. Do your due diligence to make sure the area of study you select aligns with who you are, your personal mission, and your career goals.
- Once you have selected your institution and decided on your area of study, take accountability of planning out your class schedule. Classes should fulfill requirements, explore interests, position you for strong recommendations, and set you up for your next steps.
- Get As. As are the only grade that matters.

Pillar #2: Develop an Impressive Résumé

Earn your success based on service to others, not at the expense of others.
—H. Jackson Brown, Jr.

For a time, I went through life just existing. I did some of the things my mother told me to do. I met the basic requirements for school. I participated in the events and organizations that I had to. I would attend events that excited my friends and me. That was it. I did not participate in any extracurricular activities in high school. Outside of school, the only thing I got involved with was a mentoring program my mother forced us to attend every other Saturday. If it were up to me, I would have just hung out with friends and played video games. Everything changed when I started *The Academic Hustle*.

In this section you will learn:

- What you can do outside of class to prepare you for your career.
- How to get recognized for the work you do.
- The best way to keep track of your involvements.

When I began my academic hustle, I knew scholarships were awarded to those with good grades and community service experience. So, that is where I started. What began as a mission to get school paid for, turned into a passion for empowering my community. I enjoyed making a change in my neighborhood so much that I began to join the organizations that I did community service for. When I realized that I wanted to get things done in a certain way, I got on the executive board of these organizations. It was then my responsibility to organize events and activities that would benefit my community. I fell in love with the ability to come up with an idea and then pull the people and resources together to make it happen. Doing that repeatedly transformed my understanding of life. I became a leader.

Leadership is the process of bringing people together to accomplish something. This simple process creates our society. Schools, events, businesses, organizations, activities, products, and services are all the results of leadership. For example, a group of friends and I wanted to go to New Orleans to help with the Hurricane Katrina relief efforts, so we raised funds and organized a trip during our spring break. I wanted to learn martial arts, so we started a martial arts club on campus. I desired to travel abroad, so I joined a humanitarian trip to Haiti. All these things were fun ideas that became reality when I decided to join with others to make them happen. The more I did, the more I wanted to do. Before I started doing things, I never saw myself as or believed I could be a "leader." The whole idea of joining an organization like student government and getting into a leadership position wasn't even a thought in my mind. But, when I did it, I loved it. I kept doing more and more and gaining wonderful experiences.

Little did I know, I was building quite an impressive résumé. I did not realize how valuable my experiences were until I started to win awards. I saw people raise their eyebrows when I shared what I was doing. When I got into the working world, I realized I was a much more valuable person than many of my peers because I knew how to lead teams, organize events, and get things done. Those experiences in undergrad literally transformed me into a different person and equipped me with skills and insights few people had.

When you go after opportunities, people will want to see what you have done. They are going to ask for your résumé or a list of activities. Too many students go to school thinking that getting a degree is enough. It's not. Employers and selection committees look for candidates who have experience and a full, well-balanced résumé than those who just graduated, Keep that in mind as you navigate life. What can you do to make your résumé impressive?

Selection committees prioritize well-rounded qualifications. To ensure a great résumé, you must be involved with activities of significance. The more remarkable, or out of the ordinary the activities are, the better.

So how do you become awesome? **Get involved and be impressive!** But don't just get involved in anything. Be strategic. Ideally, you want to make sure what you do is aligned with where you want to go. For example, if you want to become an accountant, which is better, being a part of the garden society or business society? Business society, yes? Should you be secretary or treasurer? Treasurer. Just by being involved, and especially getting on the leadership board, you are doing something out of the ordinary. As treasurer, you are gaining your first experience in accounting and utilizing some of your newfound skills. Most people do not get involved in activities and even fewer are in leadership positions. If you do this, you will stand out. And if you do things that are impressive, people will recognize.

Experience-Building Activities

For the sake of trying to keep this simple, I am going to categorize everything you do outside of class as "extracurricular" activities. These range from work experience to studying abroad.

Extracurricular activities are a huge part of what makes school a school. The sports, clubs, student organizations, and many other activities give life to a school. Many schools are distinguished by what they offer outside of classes (sports, conferences, debate teams, research, etc.). That isn't just a coincidence. While classes are the foundation and one of the most important parts of getting an education, extracurricular activities provide you with the opportunity to gain valuable experience.

Extracurricular activities are great opportunities for you to develop as a professional. They provide the following:

1. **Insight and exposure –** As you get involved, you will become exposed to many new things. You will literally be working in a specific field and learning what that is all about.

2. **Hands-on experience –** Activities get you out of the books and into the real world. The more you spend time DOING things, the more experience you will develop.

3. **Skills –** When you constantly organize events, fundraise, and lead meetings, you become better at them. Those things develop into skills that make you more valuable.

4. **Résumé building –** Almost everything you DO can be put on a résumé. It is YOUR list of activities and experiences. If it is relevant to the job, you can put whatever you have done on there.

5. **Expand your network and develop more relationships –** This is a very significant part of getting involved. You begin to meet people who like what you like doing and are in the same field as you. These relationships open the door to countless opportunities for you.

Most importantly, extracurricular activities are FUN! For example, being a part of the Student Government Association (SGA) and having the ability to plan almost any event or activity you want with friends using other people's money is awesome. Want to go on leadership retreats? Plan a block party? Have a forum about what it means to be a boyfriend or girlfriend? Want to get backstage passes and access to almost any celebrity that comes to campus? SGA is just one of the many great student organizations that gives you those opportunities and privileges. Sports, concerts, and parties are not the only activities you can do at school and have fun. Perhaps you would like to see a speakers' series where some of the more well-known people in your field come to talk to the university about their new books and philosophies. If what you want is not at your school, then be the one to start it. Your résumé would look even better if you founded a thriving student organization. Anybody can get in a position and be the status quo just doing what the last person did. Creating something new while in that position, like a speakers' series, is how you create a legacy.

Another great thing about extracurricular activities is that many of them are free. Some cost and others will pay you. Whatever the cost, these activities are critical to your post-graduation plans.

Get Involved

Taking advantage of extracurricular activities is simple; you just have to get involved. There are a host of activities that fall under the umbrella of extracurricular activities; here are the most popular categories:

1. Work
2. Volunteer
3. Programs

Each category offers a wide spectrum. As you figure out what you should do, and to what category it may fall in, think about getting involved by:

1. Doing things you enjoy or are interested in

2. Being strategic about what will give you the insight, experience, and/or network for what you want to do post-graduation

For those unsure of what they want to do concerning a major and a career path, extracurricular activities are the BEST way to try things out without making serious commitments. You can go from one activity to the next until you find something you enjoy. If you have an idea about what you want to do, get involved with an activity in that field. Explore it. You will come across opportunities to meet and work with people who may be doing what you want to do later in life. That will go a long way in helping you determine if that path is right for you.

Another significant point about getting involved is your performance. People will be watching you. Let me repeat that: **People are ALWAYS watching you.** If you don't do well or at least take care of your responsibilities, others will not want to work with you, period. To develop an impressive résumé, **get involved** and **BE IMPRESSIVE.**

Work

Work experience is one of the primary factors that employers consider when evaluating a candidate. However, it does not have to come solely from a paid job. There are a few ways you can gain valuable work experience:

1. Job
2. Work-Study
3. Internship
4. Entrepreneurship

Job

Having a job while in school will benefit your career plans if it aligns with your goals or if you are developing transferable skills. If you are thinking about being in the restaurant industry, take that job at a local restaurant. Do you want to be a flight attendant? Then becoming a hostess or a waiter may give you valuable, transferable skills for that position. Looking to become an accountant? Then look for jobs in banking, or work as a receptionist at an accountant's office. The point is you want your experience to be as close to your career prospects as possible. Remember what I stated earlier about making sure that your choices are relevant to a greater goal. Random jobs do not develop you and can even place you back a few steps. Working at a car detailing shop will do nothing for your future career as an airline pilot. We all have to do what we must to survive and take care of our family, but the more you can align your work experience with your career goals, the better.

Exercise P2.1 – Identifying Jobs in Your Career Field

Using the research you compiled in Exercise F2.5, create a list of jobs in your industry that you can do while still in school. Occupational handbooks found at your nearest library or bookstore are a great start. Also, online databases of jobs like *O*Net Online* can be great resources. Do not limit yourself by only thinking about what is currently available in your area. It's time to grow. Create a list of possibilities to do so.

Pay special attention to the job description and requirements. There may be jobs you can get outside of your industry that can give you the opportunity to develop transferable skills.

Once you have your list, contact local companies and ask them about the actual job requirements. Write as much information down as possible. Everything should be in one notebook.

Work-Study

Work-study gives you the opportunity to have a part-time job at the school. Students can earn money to cover basic costs while still focusing on school. Examples include assisting department secretaries, working at the school's library, manning the entrance to the school's gym, etc. You usually have to talk to the financial aid office or department heads to identify openings. Simply ask around about work-study opportunities and you are bound to find a few.

When taking advantage of work-study options, again, be strategic. Talk to whoever assigns the jobs and try to select something that will:

1. **Give you access –** If you get an opportunity to work in the financial aid office, you may be able to gain insight into how to secure money to pay for school. If working for the president's office, you may gain access to all the powerful people who come to campus.

2. **Provide good benefits –** Working in the café may come with free meals. Working in your major's department can give you the chance to be the first to know about opportunities available to students.

3. **Develop a skill or gain experience and exposure –** You may be able to work in the media center and learn production or at the gym and practice training others.

The point is to weigh the pros and cons of the work-study opportunities that may be available and pick the one that will be the most beneficial to you.

I had a work-study job my freshman year in the sociology department. I mainly assisted a professor, Dr. Cynthia Hewitt, with planning events and programs. I learned how to develop flyers, reserve rooms, and organize events. It was a great opportunity because I got acquainted with the top students in the department and all of the professors. At the time, Dr. Hewitt was developing a student service-learning trip to Haiti called G.E.N.E.S.I.S. and I was helping with many of the programmatic details. Guess who was one of the first people considered for the limited-access trip? Not only did my work-study position lead to my first trip out of the country, but it gave me the opportunity to hang out with one of my favorite artists at the time, Wyclef Jean, in Haiti!

Exercise P2.2 – Identifying Work-Study Sites

At the very beginning of the school year or right before it starts,

1. Ask the secretaries of various departments within your school about any work-study jobs they know about.
2. List all the work-study opportunities that align with your career development goals.
3. Find out who is responsible for selecting students and how students are selected.
4. Write all that information down in one notebook.
5. Prepare your presentation (discussed in Pillar 4) for the authority over the work-study hires.

Internships

Internships give you the opportunity to be directly exposed to what it means to work in a specific industry and provide you with great hands-on experience. They look appealing on your résumé and can put you in the position to get a recommendation from someone in your field. Internships also show the people you are working for that you are an ideal candidate for the next job opening. Interns are usually paid much lower than the average worker in the same position or they may be unpaid; however, the pay is not why you should do internships.

I am not a fan of unpaid internships. I strongly believe people should be paid for the value they create. I would only do an unpaid internship if it would give me tremendous access to information or people who will basically guarantee me a job or improved career outcomes. Companies know the value of good workers and they will pay for outstanding people. However, some companies will take advantage of your time and these are the ones you probably don't want to work for. There are plenty of paid internships, so make sure an unpaid internship is worth it. Remember, internships are not about the money. They are about getting exposure, gaining experience, building your résumé, and developing your network.

The best time to take advantage of internships while in school is during your breaks, especially summer breaks. If you are clear regarding your goals, then working an internship while in school can give you work experience that could potentially set you up for a job immediately after graduation.

To get the most out of internships, focus on doing those that are in the field you want to get into or thinking about getting into. Internships are a great way to test a future job out. When you get there, be sure to excel in every way possible by making great impressions on your colleagues and creating good relationships.

Before you graduate, **you should have completed AT LEAST one internship**. Start planning and strategizing *immediately* about where you will be interning and when.

I stumbled into politics after getting involved on campus and, consequently, running for SGA President. When the opportunity came up (through one of my mentors from the 100 Black Men of South Florida) to intern on Capitol Hill for Congressman Kendrick Meek, I jumped at it. This opportunity was offered by the Congressional Black Caucus Internship Program. I developed briefings, attended committee meetings, and conducted legislative research for my hometown's congressional representative. I was surrounded by the people who make the laws of the land and are always on TV. I had opportunities to talk with them and share ideas. It was an unique experience. However, after interning on Capitol Hill, I realized politics on a national level was not for me. It was too intense and intrusive on an individual's personal life and beliefs.

Exercise P2.2 – Identifying Internships

Using the keywords from your research thus far, begin to conduct an online search for internships in your industry. Use each of the keywords you developed and attach the word "internships" at the end when conducting an online search. For example, "engineering internships," "civil engineering internships," and "mechanical engineering internships." Note all your options.

Next, identify the major businesses, organizations, and associations in your industry and check their websites for internships. Note each opportunity.

Entrepreneurship

Starting your own business can be an excellent way to gain insight and experience in your field. What you will need to learn about the industry to create a successful business can be eye opening. Moreover, the work ethic and business acumen of a successful entrepreneur is impressive.

If you are learning a trade, you can start out by doing small jobs for people that may not require certifications. If you plan to be a graphic designer, design flyers and logos for people. If you want to be a computer engineer, fix people's computers in your spare time. If you want to be a teacher, tutor students. The possibilities are endless and they await you. The point is to use your time wisely to gain work experience that empowers your career and money-making potential.

Volunteering

Many people stray away from the idea of volunteering to their own disadvantage. People tend to think that doing things for free is a waste of time. They are wrong. Volunteering gives you all the benefits of work experience, without the pay. Through volunteering, you gain hands-on experience for your career, access insight and exposure to your industry, develop valuable transferable skills, build your résumé, and, most importantly, expand your network. I can guarantee the Who's Who in your field are involved in multiple volunteer organizations. Volunteering is crucial to career development.

Most volunteer activities are the result of organizations and associations that come together around a specific cause. They range from community service organizations, professional associations, and interest clubs. They are great places take part in a wide range and meet people in your desired field.

As a lesson for your life and career, always be a part of at least one organization that will set you up within your industry or for your next step. People who are involved in these organizations are usually those that are in the know, the people in power positions. As you become a part of these organizations and their activities, you will become a more valuable person. Be strategic and get involved in what is best for your next step.

Strategic Involvements

There are a few ways to identify the right volunteer organization. First, think about your career development. What do you want to do later in life? Are you looking to get into a specific field or industry? If so, look for an organization that has something to do with your future career choice. It should be something that will give you the exposure, skills, qualities, experiences, or network in the industry of your choice. Begin by visiting your student activities office or organizational fair. These will give you ideas about on-campus organizations. Off-campus organizations can be just as, if not more valuable. When searching for off-campus organizations, ask people in your field or do an online search. Conducting an online search is as simple as putting your career field or interest area in a search engine and adding "organization," "association," or "club."

Suppose someone wants to become a biomedical engineer. What he or she wants to do is identify volunteer organizations on or off campus that are in the health care, biology, medical, or engineering fields and get involved with them. If you want to become a lawyer, investigate getting involved with the debate club, pre-law society, or a political studies club. Remember to be strategic and get involved with the organization that will give you the most for the time you invest in it.

Once you have identified organizations to get involved with, do the following:

1. **Check them out** – Attend their meetings, go to an event or two, talk to the members and leadership. Do not commit on the spot;instead, shop around. Narrow your choices and identify one or a few that draw your interest.

2. **Join –** After you've made your choice, make sure you are a member, so you can put that on your résumé.

3. **Get involved and perform well –** This will build your reputation and create relationships that may open the doors to many other possibilities.

4. **Look for opportunities to be involved in something that will look good on your résumé –** At the end of the day, those involved in your next step will evaluate you based on what is on paper and the experiences you can share. Think strategically about what committees you join and what tasks you undertake.

5. **Seek out opportunities to develop a skill and gain exposure –** Try planning an event for the group or being the go-to person for a certain aspect of the organization. If you are into marketing, take over the marketing of the organization. Do whatever you can to build your experience. Nervous? This is the ideal time to make mistakes and learn from them.

6. **Get in a leadership position –** Explaining the benefits of this takes a whole section. See below.

7. **Make friends and acquaintances –** Remember your peers will be people of significance later in life. Be sure to establish connections now that can benefit you later.

8. **Try to accomplish something major –**Stand out. Contribute to the organization or cause. Make a mark. Start a new initiative. Do a big event. Make news. Not only will this look impressive in your list of qualifications, people will recognize how your presence influenced the organization.

If you have looked on campus and have not found something you would like to be a part of, then start your own organization. I founded two organizations while in school. I have always had an interest in health, fitness, and martial arts and was disappointed that my school did not have a club. I pulled together some other students on campus who were also interested and founded the Health, Fitness, & Martial Arts club at Morehouse.

I also wanted an organization where the men on campus could hang out, plan events, and empower each other to become better students. Therefore, I attended the national conference for Student African American Brotherhood, learned what it took, sought out support, and helped found the chapter at Morehouse College. I served as the personal development chair and helped the organization expand from our original fifteen members to over fifty. We traveled to conferences, planned events, and had a lot of fun. As the personal development chair, I had a platform to do workshops on school success, and now, over ten years later, I am writing a book about it and speaking across the country.

Leadership

Leadership is one of the most transformational things you can do in life. Too many times it is made out to be much more than it really is, as if you must be born into it. That was definitely not the case for me.

I started being a "leader" when I joined the executive board of the Morehouse Sociological Association as a secretary. I did it to put something on my résumé for scholarships. It soon became more than that. As I fulfilled my duties, I learned how to develop proposals for events by working with the president at the time, Yven Destin. I did not care for the work, but I handled my responsibilities. From that initial position, I went after other positions on executive boards—again, to build my résumé. For the next three years of college, I served in every executive board position. It was not all smooth-sailing. I had my fair share of failures. For instance, I was never acknowledged as a "good" leader. One of the biggest blows to my self-esteem was not being elected President of the Student African American Brotherhood Morehouse Chapter, an organization I founded. Someone I recruited was elected by other people who I also recruited! In a situation like this, many would have sulked and sworn off leadership roles and people in general. As noted above, I was on a mission to create an organization for men to empower each other. The mission was most important, not my ego. Therefore, I served as personal development chair until I graduated. One thing is certain: it would have been impossible to grow in this aspect of my professional life without pursuing such positions. Now, after over 10 years of serving in leadership positions, people continually say that I am "a natural born leader!" Nothing could be further from the truth.

Every leader is made by how they handle their responsibilities. Great leaders handle their duties in an extraordinary fashion. Poor leaders have toxic, morale-destroying meltdowns and do not take care of their obligations. The foundation of leadership is in taking care of responsibilities and doing so offers quite a few benefits:

- **Résumé Building** – Employers like to see leadership positions and accomplishments on a résumé. It tells the employer that you know how to handle and complete duties and that you have organizational, management, and communication skills.
- **Expanding Network –** As a leader, you are a point person in the organization. People have to come to you to get certain things done. Moreover, to make things happen, you must work with others. Working with someone is the best way to expand your network and you become more than just a name. People get a glimpse of who you are. They will remember you and can recall such experiences if they ever have to recommend you for something.
- **Developing Organizational and Management Skills –**The higher up you are in a company, the more organizational and management skills you will need. Volunteering gives you an opportunity to practice and hone these skills.
- **Improving Communication Skills –** Clear communication is the lifeblood of a team. Leaders must perfect this skill because they are responsible for leading the team and providing clarity. Moreover, leaders have plenty of occasions to practice communicating because they constantly have to speak on behalf of the organization.
- **Enhancing Emotional Intelligence –** When you constantly have to work with people and get them to complete tasks despite all the things happening in their lives, you begin to develop a perception of how others feel and can react accordingly. This emotional intelligence is a powerful skill for navigating through life.
- **Feeling of Accomplishment –** The feeling of accomplishment that goes along with planning a successful activity, hearing praise about how well an

event went, or hearing someone telling you how your efforts positively impacted their lives is fulfilling. To see an idea manifest into an actual campaign or event is empowering. You begin to recognize that you can actually make a tangible impact on the world.

- **Having Fun and Creating Friends –** While leadership does have its sour moments, people enjoy leading because it is fun. Through the process, you get to know people and can create lifelong friends.

Leadership has quite a few benefits that balance out the not-so-fun responsibilities. However, those benefits correlate to how well the responsibilities are handled. Become a leader, handle your responsibilities, and watch the perks come your way.

Exercise P2.4 – Identifying Volunteer Opportunities

1. Review the list of on-campus organizations and activities.

2. If you do not see something you want to get involved in, write down some organizations or activities you would like create.

3. Also, list every volunteer opportunity you can imagine in your career field.

Review your list of interest and conduct an online search for organizations and associations in your field. Note them.

Programs

Programs are little known activities in college that can provide tremendous opportunities for advancement. They cover a wide range of activities. It is hard to categorize them. As you have seen in the above example, the Congressional Black Caucus Internships Program, was a program and internship rolled into one. When I mention programs, I am referring to any organized opportunity that exposes you to a specific field or experience. Here are a few I will review:

1. Research and Summer Programs
2. Fellowships
3. Events & Conferences
4. Study Abroad

There are many programs that disguise themselves as internships, study abroad experiences, summer opportunities, etc. If you participate in one of those programs that alone will make you a distinctive candidate. Ask around your department, your teachers, or fellow classmates to find out about as many as possible. There are almost always additional programs that schools offer to enhance their student body experiences. Be a part of the select few that participate in these activities and stand out from the competition.

Research and Summer Programs

If you want to go to graduate school, you should consider getting involved in a research program. These programs give you the skills, insight, and network that will make you a competitive candidate. Moreover, if you ever wanted to study a specific subject or issue, these programs will pay you to do it.

The National Institute of Mental Health Career Opportunities in Research (NIHM-COR) Honors Undergraduate Research Training Program was one of the best programs I ever participated in. It provided 75 percent of tuition, a monthly stipend of over $900, research training classes, funding for trips to conferences, and support from mentors who let us work in their research labs. NIHM-COR was one of the most supportive and transforming programs I have ever participated in. Dr. Margaret Weber-Levine and Dr. Karen Brakke facilitated a program that trained groups of about twenty students for two years in advanced research methods. In our group were some of the top scholars at our institution and in our departments. We conducted research and presented our findings across the country. The financial, staff, and group support was unmatched by any other program at my school. It was *the* premier program to support a student's career development at Morehouse. My research, writing, and presentation skills grew exponentially because of the countless hours of classes, training, one-on-one mentorship, and support from my peers. I found out about the program by checking a bulletin board in my department and then talking to the department secretary and a few professors about it. The Atlanta University Consortium's (AUC) NIMH-COR program is directly responsible for the research that laid the foundation of the book you have in your hands.

Another program I was involved in was the University of California – Berkeley Summer Research Opportunities Program. I received an all-expense paid trip to Berkeley, California where I lived rent-free in a beautiful dormitory for international students located on the side of a hill that overlooked all of the Bay area for almost three months. I had a research mentor, Dr. Jarralynne Agee, who encouraged me to combine my love for self-help and culture into my summer project.

Dr. Agee guided me in conducting a qualitative analysis on the qualities and characteristics of high-achieving men. I interviewed men who were in the top of their fields (judges, doctors, directors, professors) and asked them questions about their life, how they overcame some of the obstacles to success noted in academic literature (theories like academic disidentification, stereotype threat, culture of poverty, and oppositional culture), and what advice they had for others. Hearing wisdom from so many high-achieving men in various careers was life-changing. I analyzed the interviews using a thematic content analysis to identify the common characteristics and methods to their success. After countless fourteen-hour days and many sleepless nights, I produced a research project that gave me my first national honor. In 2007, I presented part of my research, *An Analysis of Major Theories on Academic Underachievement in Relation to High-Achieving African American Men,* at the NIMH – COR Conference in Albuquerque, New Mexico (a fully funded trip that included a multi-night hotel stay, cash each day—also known as per diem—spectacular dinners, and even a train ride up a mountain that gave us a bird's eye view of the city of Albuquerque) and won the Wayne S. Fenton Undergraduate Research Scholar Award. That research project also laid the foundation for the study I did on high-academic achievers. As you can imagine, that work is being used in the writing of this book.

My involvement in research and summer programs was one of the most transformational experiences of my college experience.

Fellowships

Fellowships are one of the most distinctive honors someone can receive. Fellowships come with a stipend (i.e. money), acceptance into an exclusive group pursuing a mutual practice or area of knowledge, and some type of training.

One of the fellowships I received in as an undergrad was the United Negro College Fund (UNCF) Mellon Mays Undergraduate Fellowship. Its mission is to increase the number of underrepresented minority groups who pursue PhDs. I got involved because I had a dream of becoming a professor. The UNCF Mellon Mays Fellowship was the top program in my area to help minorities get a PhD. We participated in numerous trainings, including an intensive six-week summer program focused on training participants in research and preparing us for graduate school.

Dr. Bilal Mansa Mark King served as my research mentor and I was given thousands of dollars in travel, research, and book stipends to support my development. That support was funneled into my research on high-academic achievers. I spent two years conducting a mixed method (quantitative and qualitative) analysis of students who received over 3.3 GPA in high school or college. I interviewed and collected data on 24 students asking questions such as:

- What are some of the skills, strategies, and techniques you have used to maintain over a 3.3 cumulative GPA?
- What are the main personality traits that you believe helped you excel in school? What about attitudes?
- Could you tell me some habits or strategies that helped you excel in school?
- Do you believe that environment influences your outlook on education? If so, how?
- Please list at least three of the following that have contributed to your success: books/poems/songs/quotes/ movies/TV series and/or personal philosophies of life.

My participants were the top students and leaders on campus. Some graduated at the top of their departments, many were Phi Beta Kappa (arguably, the most prestigious honor society in the nation). Others went on to graduate school at Ivy League institutions, won prestigious awards like the Fulbright, worked on Wall Street, and even participated in the Olympics! I learned a lot from my research subjects. The papers and presentations I produced from the project won quite a few awards, put more money in my pocket, and laid the foundation for *The Academic Hustle*. Shout out to Dr. Cynthia Neal Spence and Ms. Ada Jackson for believing in me and pushing the limits of the fellowship to support my dreams! I promise I will get that PhD!

Exercise P2.6 – Identifying Fellowships

Using the keywords from your research so far, begin to conduct an online search for fellowships in your industry. Use each of the keywords you developed and attach "fellowships" at the end of it when conducting an online search—for example, "science fellowships," "business fellowships," and "mechanical fellowships." Note all your options.

Identify organizations, associations, corporations and foundations in your field. Peruse their websites for any opportunities. Note them.

Study Abroad

If I had to choose the most powerful extracurricular activity, it would be studying abroad. When you are in a place that has a different language, culture, and way of life, it changes you. It is simply amazing. I highly recommend studying abroad to anyone and everyone. There are basically three types of study abroad experiences:

- **Student Exchange –** Some schools have partnerships with other schools where you can attend classes at another university. If you have plans to go to a university for graduate school or wanted to take a specific class, then these programs are invaluable. There are a lot of schools that have exchange programs with other schools in the nation. I highly recommend taking part in an exchange with a school out of the country.
- **Foreign Trips –** These are programs that take you to a place for anywhere between five to thirty days. They are good opportunities to see another country. Sometimes they offer class credit. I am not too fond of these programs because they usually have a lot of out-of-the-pocket costs that catch up to you on the back end. Plus,

the experience is too short. If you really want to learn a language, live in another country, and get to know a culture get into a program that will have you there for more than ten weeks. The major exception to this is Semester at Sea, which is a balance between a foreign trip and study abroad. During Semester at Sea, you are on a boat, literally traveling the world, for at least ten weeks. You get to stay in multiple countries for a few days each. You only get to spend a little time in each place, and the experience of seeing so many different countries and learning about them while on a boat is phenomenal. It was a dream of mine that I did not realize. Hopefully, you can.

- **Study Abroad –** To me, study abroad is an experience of over ten weeks outside of your country that is coupled with some type of academic training. I would advise all students to study abroad at some point during their time as a student. These programs are an impressive addition to your résumé and will provide you with experiences that you will cherish for the rest of your life. Moreover, many of the highly competitive schools and jobs love people with experience abroad. We are in a globalized world and foreign experience is valuable. Make it a priority to figure out how to do this. There are plenty of programs and scholarships that will pay for you to study abroad. Also, ask anyone who has done one of these about the impact it has made on his or her life and if there was much "studying" during the program.

My study abroad experience came from the Penn State University Minority Health International Research Training (PSU-MHIRT) Program run by Dr. Gary King. It was a summer program that exposed minorities to the public health field through international research training. Our introduction and training for the program took place in Paris for a week. Yes, you heard that correctly. I had an all-expense paid trip to Paris for a week to get "introduced and trained." We were then sent to different places across the world. I was sent to Tanzania to study adolescent smoking in Dares Salaam for the summer. It was the most powerful experience of my life. I can write an entire book about all the life-changing moments I had. I did my work and made sure to experience the culture and explore the land. Once I completed my project and presented my research at the end of the program, we flew back to Paris for a week to debrief as a group.

In addition to expenses being paid, we received a $3,000 living stipend. My group rented out a condo on the beach and hired a maid. It was awesome. If you don't seek experiences like that, you are truly missing out. I applied to the program immediately after I found out about it through one of my professors, Dr. Sinead Young, who was leading the trip for the colleges in my area.

Exercise P2.7 – Identifying Study Abroad Opportunities

Visit your school's study abroad office and your major and minor's departments to find out about these opportunities.

Events & Conferences

All industries, fields, and professions have events and conferences. These events and conferences bring people together and provide a platform to share insights from the field. They are great places to meet people, network, and gain insight into your industry.

Events can range from community service activities, to a panel discussion, to a full-scale gala. This is a very broad category. Conferences are a little more specific. They are large events that organizations plan around a certain theme. Conferences usually bring together experts in the field and a ton of people interested in that topic.

Events and conferences have two major advantages:

1. **Opportunities to connect with leaders in your field –** The movers and shakers in the field usually attend these events and conferences. You could not only hear what the experts in your field are thinking, but also give yourself the opportunity to connect with them.

2. **Conduct workshops and presentations –** Events and conferences are platforms for people in the field to share insight. You can be one of those people and that is a significant achievement to put on your résumé.

To make the best of the time at these events, here are some tips:

1. **Attend:** Go to as many of these as possible. You will be amazed at what opportunities present themselves.

2. **Take notes:** At these events, people have put a lot of time into thinking about what they want to share during their presentation. Many of them are experts in their field or on their topic. Do not let such valuable information be lost. Capture it so that you can refer to it when the time comes to use their insight.

3. **Network:** All types of people attend events. Events are a central location for everyone interested in the idea to congregate. Use this to your advantage to build your network within the field. You never know who you will meet.

4. **Stand out:** At these events, you will be one of many. To improve your chances of meeting key people, winning awards, or making great connections, you must make an effort to stand out.

When I was in undergrad, I attended quite a few events and conferences. Even now, I constantly attend them. They are a natural part of professional life and great resources for career development. My first job out of college was the result of attending and standing out at a conference.

How to Stand Out

People remember the best. People remember the popular. People remember the different. At events and conferences, people remember the master of ceremonies. They notice the speakers. They take note of the people who ask interesting or engaging questions. They can identify with the best presenters. They observe people everyone else gathers around. They see who receives recognition and wins awards. If you want people to remember and recognize you, strive to do things that will make you stand out.

In the spring of 2009, a few months before graduation, I made it a point to attend the Southeastern Undergraduate Sociological Symposium (SEUSS) for a few reasons. First, the keynote speaker, Dr. Darren Woodruff, was my research mentor's mentor from his time at American Institute for Research, the largest social science research institute in the nation. I wanted to make sure I connected with him because working at a research institute would strengthen my application to almost any of the top PhD programs in the nation. Second, I had been working on my high-academic achievers research project. The conference was one of the last big events in my field where I could present my work as a social science undergraduate researcher. Being a presenter would make me stand out more than an attendee and an award-winner would place me as one of the top presenters. Also, winning an award at a conference with the "Who's Who" is equal to a strong recommendation from everyone at the conference. It gives you great access to almost anyone in attendance. Moreover, it looks awesome on a résumé. Also, by thinking strategically about where I wanted to go (research job → grad school → professor), I realized that shining at this conference would help me on quite a few levels. My goal was to win.

Before the conference, I put in countless hours to develop a top-notch paper to present at the conference. During the conference, I made sure I asked at least one thoughtful question during every session. I engaged the presenters and as many conference participants as possible. I was intentional about introducing myself and speaking to all the conference organizers and anyone that looked somewhat important. I practiced my presentation over and over to make sure I did the best presentation of my life at the time. During the closing session, my work paid off. I won the 1st Place Paper Award for Excellence in Undergraduate Research.

While at the conference, I made sure my research mentor, Dr. Bilal Mansa Mark King, introduced me to Dr. Woodruff. Throughout the conference, we talked and even had tea together. We spoke about potential job opportunities, which led to an informal interview with him. After the conference, I followed up with Dr. Woodruff, submitted my application, and got a job. While everyone else was stressing about the economy and the lack of jobs (this was during the American Great Recession where the Dean gave a speech to our graduating class saying it was the worst time to be entering the job market, in living memory) and submitting hundreds of applications, I secured mine by attending a conference and standing out.

Exercise P2.9 – Developing Your Extracurricular Master Plan

After completing the previous exercises, review all the extracurricular options that you have.

1. Identify at least one volunteer organization for your career and one within your interest area (no more than four).

2. Select no more than two organizations where you can get a leadership position.

3. Put on your calendar at least two events you will attend each month.

4. Arrange to attend at least one conference a year.

5. Review your job, work-study, internships, fellowships, summer, and research program options.

6. Considering your financial needs, prioritize which would be more beneficial to your career development and how you may be able to arrange them around your graduation.

7. Once all the above has been taken care of, see if you can fit study abroad opportunities into your plan.

8. Lastly, apply!

Completing this exercise will lay a strong foundation for your career. Following through on your plan will transform you in ways you never thought were possible.

Win Awards and Get Recognized

Receiving honors and awards are great additions to your résumé. They also expand your access to influential people. The funny thing is that it really isn't that hard to obtain these honors and awards. Most people just do not intentionally go after them. The people who win awards are usually the ones who do. Please understand that what is meant by going after awards is not to humiliate yourself by begging and sucking up to people. This is about shining so undeniably, that you are impossible to ignore.

To win an award you need to meet the criteria and be outstanding. The only thing that is "hard" about getting accepted or winning an award is doing what it takes to meet the criteria and standing out. It requires work to win those awards. If you want to win an award, you need to:

1. Find out the criteria or evaluation protocol by contacting the award committee.

2. Identify the selection committee. This may be tricky. It may be as simple as asking the award committee, finding out who served on the selection committee last year by asking around, or deducing the most likely people. Usually, the selection committee is composed of the organizers of the event or leaders of the organization. Sometimes they are prominent invited guests.

3. Figure out how to be outstanding in the committee's eyes. Try to find out their likes and dislikes by finding information about them. Ask around. Do research online to identify things like their background, work experience, and interests. See if you can identify the rubric they are using to evaluate candidates and make sure you know the mission, vision, and values of the organization.

4. Introduce yourself to the selection committee and anyone of significance. Have an engaging conversation with them, if possible.

5. Talk to previous recipients of the award.

6. Perform to the best of your abilities, ensuring that you include the award criteria, likes of the selection committee and tips from previous awardees in what you do.

Outside of scholarships, my first national award was the Wayne S. Fenton Undergraduate Research Scholar Award given at the NIMH-COR conferences in 2007. At the opening of the conferences, the officials talked about their award for the undergraduate researcher that conducted stellar research and presented at the conference. But it wasn't just about the presentation. They wanted to award it to someone who stood out and interacted during the conference. I made a note of everything they said about the award, the people on stage, and anyone that looked like they were a part of the organizing committee of the conference. During the conference, I attended every session I could, especially those with the most members of the selection committee. While in each session, I listened attentively, asked thoughtful questions, and engaged with the presenter afterward. I made it a point of mine to interact with the people who attended each session and invited them to my presentation. When I gave my presentation, the room was full, and I did the best I could. I spoke to every person I could identify on the selection committee and made sure they knew my name and the research project I was presenting. Even though I was strategic about everything, I did it all in a pleasant manner, enjoying each conversation. When we had the closing ceremony, those that were wishing for the award were praying. I knew I had it in the bag. They called my name and I walked up in front of hundreds of people to claim what I had worked for.

If you are going after an Olympic gold medal, you have to understand the rules and regulations to qualify, what your judges are evaluating you on, who your judges are and what they like to see, what have past gold medalist done to win, and how to stand out from your competition. Once you understand these characteristics, do what you must do. It requires work, but if you do what it takes, you will win.

Exercise P2.10 – Plan to Win Awards

Upon getting involved with any type of institution, immediately identify the awards and recognitions given. Search for them within your school, department, volunteer opportunities, jobs, programs, newspapers, events, and conferences. Learn what it takes to win and be intentional about going after them.

You may not win them all, but the process of trying will make you an award-winner.

Create a Master Résumé

As you get involved, be sure to note what you are doing. I started doing this when I learned about the curriculum vitae (CV). A CV is a more in-depth résumé that contains almost everything that you have done professionally. People in academia have them to list their publications and presentations. I got the idea of including all my extracurricular activities when I started putting my presentations on my résumé. I had the following categories:

- Work experience
- Research experience
- Presentations
- Publications
- Leadership and volunteer activities
- Honors & Awards

As I got involved, I put EVERYTHING in this document. After each experience, I created bullet points that detailed my responsibilities and any accomplishments. I was sure to emphasize any impact I made with numbers and statistics. When I needed to apply to something, I would pick and choose what to put on the résumé or CV I would submit. We will talk more about tailoring your résumé when discussing pillar four. The point is, make sure you collect what you do and keep it in one place. Make it easy to share what you have done.

Exercise P2.11 – Develop Your Master Résumé

Always have a master résumé ready to tailor at a moment's notice. Here's how to create and maintain one:

1. Search online for a résumé template that you like.
2. Fill it in each of the above categories with *everything* you have done.

3. Create sections for the activities you are currently doing.

4. Make a point to update this master résumé after every accomplishment or at the end of each semester.

Keeping an updated résumé is also an accountability tool. Each semester you are reporting to yourself what you have accomplished. Being able to see it on paper can be extremely motivating.

Follow your passions in a strategic manner, making sure that when you get involved, you really get involved. Take on responsibilities and do your best to shine. Try to plan an event or execute your responsibilities to the best of your abilities. You want to be able to write about accomplishments.

As you get involved, look for any awards, honors, or recognitions and be intentional about going after them. Try to get on the dean's list, try to get into that honor society, do as much as you can to make yourself look good. This isn't a shoulder shrugging, "aw shucks" kind of vibe. You don't have to creep everyone out by being obsessive, but do see it as a job in and of itself. These are the things that competitive candidates do.

All successful people do more than just work or go to school. You will see them on boards, a part of associations, engaged in the community, or doing something outside of work and school. That isn't a coincidence. To be more, you must do more (and be smart about it). Be sure to get involved.

Takeaways

- Securing a degree and excelling in your educational program is not enough. You must develop your experience.
- The best way to develop your experience and build your résumé is to get involved strategically.
- Strategically select jobs, work-study opportunities, internships, and entrepreneurial endeavors that align with your career goals.
- Volunteer organizations and the leadership opportunities they provide are essential to professional development. Almost every high-achieving professional is involved with some type of volunteer organization.
- Research programs, summer programs, fellowships, study abroad experiences, events, and conferences can provide life-changing experiences that supercharge your career advancement. Take full advantage of them.
- Don't just get involved. Stand out! Win awards! There is a science to doing this.
- Document everything that you do in résumé format—your master résumé. You will use the information in this document to quickly create tailor-made résumé for opportunities you are applying to.

Pillar #3: Establish a Network of High Net Worth

The ends you serve that are selfish will take you no further than yourself; but the ends you serve that are for all, in common, will take you even into eternity.

—Marcus Garvey

Humans are very social creatures. Everything that you do will involve interactions with people. If you make these interactions pleasant, it will take you a long way in life. It is the key to networking.

In this section you'll learn:

- Why it is important to create genuine connections with the people who cross your path.
- How to work a room.
- Who are the people that can assist you in funding your education.
- The steps to securing strong recommendations and references.

It's About How You Connect With People

Everything in our society involves people. Always remember they are human just like you and me. They have a family, interests, likes, and dislikes. They hang out, laugh, joke and think. They evaluate people. They eat, sleep, and poop. No matter how old or young they are, what positions of authority they are in, they all do these things. Understanding this fact will take you far in life.

We tend to disregard others that are not our friends or family. We don't give them the respect they deserve. We usually look at people in a transactional way - what they can do for us. Whether that is ringing up our groceries, teaching our classes, or being our boss, we tend to overlook the fact that they want to be acknowledged and respected, just as we do. If you truly understand that people are human just like you and you treat them how you would like to be treated, then you know all you need to know about excelling in human relations. It's amazing how something so basic is so hard to implement.

I've always had serious problems relating to people. As a child, I spent a lot of time taking care of my lil brother. I didn't have many friends. The people I played with were always younger than me and the people I hung out with were always older. Also, I had a serious problem with trusting people.

In my community, interactions were kept on a surface level. You laughed, you joked, but you never really got personal. You rarely exposed yourself. You kept your distance from people because you did not want to be hurt. As a man, you didn't talk about your problems or feelings. If someone wasn't your friend or family, then they didn't matter.

For most of my life, I lived by that code and I kept to myself. I was never the popular kid so, to be recognized, I would be the clown. That was all I felt that I had to work with. There was nothing special about me back then, no noteworthy achievements or involvements. I was just there, blinking and breathing, trying to figure out how to deal with people. Yes, the author of this book was socially awkward, something I still struggle with even today. I sometimes don't know what to say or how to act, even around my friends and family.

After years of practice, many have told me that I am a "people person." That one is more hilarious to me than the "natural born leader" compliment. I still must be very intentional about going out of my way to talk to people and make a good impression. There's a little bit of fear we all have when interacting with others. Will this person like me? What should I say? Will I say or do something embarrassing? It's a numbers game, really. You just have to put yourself out there. To excel in human relations, you must overcome this fear and engage people constantly.

I have read a lot about creating good relationships with people and have put what I learned into practice. My recipe for excelling in human relations boils down to four qualities and one technique.

Qualities for Creating Good Impressions

Creating a good impression on people is largely about who you are. If you make an effort to cultivate these qualities, people will love you:

- **Be a Good Person –** Be pleasant constantly. Do good. Do right. Treat people how you would want to be treated. Never be spiteful, mean, or unkind.
- **Be Genuine –** Being genuine means not lying, not being deceptive, or not act like someone you are not. As we say in my community, "stop fakin and frontin." Be tactfully straight up with people. Try not to beat around the bush. Speak and act from your heart. Also, be open with people. Let them know your story, dreams, and struggles. People like to know who they are talking to. Also, how can people help you if they don't know what interests you?
- **Be Respectful –** Never disrespect people. Be very clear about what someone may consider disrespectful. It's not what you think, but what they believe is disrespectful. Perception is key, theirs. As a rule of thumb, acknowledge their authority, position, or who they are. Do not get loud, blatantly defy them, argue, or talk back. When someone says something, believe that they mean it.
- **Be Awesome –** Everyone likes awesome people that perform well. Do what you say you are going to do and impress others. Work hard, play hard, and live with excellence.

I guarantee you that if you cultivate these qualities and practice the techniques below, you will become a well-respected person.

Exercise P3.1 – Cultivate the Qualities of Making a Good Impression

Before every class, meeting, event, or interaction with people, affirm that you will practice these qualities. Remind yourself to practice them as you talk to people. After the interaction, take a moment to think about how well you practiced these qualities.

The Art of Conversation

The single most important technique to excelling in human relations is the art of conversation. People like to talk. When people talk, they are spending time with you. They are sharing themselves, their thoughts, experiences, and insights. This level of exchange creates bonds between people. The more time you spend with a person, the more you know about each other, and in turn, the stronger the bond between the two of you will become. Knowing how to create that bond with people will open the doors to countless opportunities of goodwill for you.

People are treasure troves of resources. Once you create a bond with someone and impress them, you can tap into their resources.

Talking to people is the first step in creating a bond with someone. The most important skill you can learn when it comes to developing a network of high net worth is learning how to carry a conversation with anyone. Learn all that you can about this skill.

Get people to talk about themselves and you're more than halfway there. People love to hear their name spoken by others. Whoever can confirm their value, engage others in their interests, get them to talk about their lives and their views, will be liked in return. This is the key to building rapport with people.

Building rapport with people is getting people to talk about their experiences, interests, and insights. The primary engaging factors are centered on how they spend their time, which is usually family, work, volunteer activities, and leisure. Talk to people about these things. Get them to share their experiences, interests, and insights and learn about their what they do with their free time. You are bound to find something you can talk about and have interest in. This is when you can hone in and your genuine interest shines which keeps you from coming off as phony. The point is to be interested in them. Get them talking, not you. Get them talking, *then* add in your experiences and thoughts... to get them to talk even more.

Power Networking

Networking is a concept you will hear a lot about throughout life, especially in the professional world. Your network can literally be your net worth. This means that the people you know and those that know you are the true estimate of your value.

Throughout time and in traditions across the world, people have always emphasized the importance of the company you keep:

Birds of a feather flock together.
Show me your friends and I'll tell you who you are.
He who walks with wise men will be wise, but the companion of fools will suffer harm
—**Proverbs 13:20**

Associate yourself with people of good quality, for it is better to be alone than to be in bad company.
—**Booker T. Washington**

The people around you can either make or break you. Choose to develop relationships with people who move you forward or whichever way the wind blows in dictating the people around you. Either way, the MOST IMPORTANT determining factor of your future is your relationships. It is your peers who mold and shape you, grant you access, and who can help you make money.

People are resources. Almost everything you see around you has been shaped by people. People are the ones who plan events, create our organizations, develop businesses, hire others, and connect you to opportunities. Therefore, it is essential that you see the value in others and make an effort to connect with them. You will feel most comfortable in situations where you bring value to the relationship in return. That is the basis of networking: connecting individuals, creating relationships, and exchanging your knowledge and resources.

Networking at Events & Conferences

Events and conferences are the best places to network. When you are at events and conferences, you will be around many people who may be connected to significant people and resources that you may need or want. When attending events or conferences be sure to do the following:

1. **Identify the people you want to meet or who should know your name:** Look through the agenda, program, or list of attendees. Think about your goals and identify the people who you think can help you get closer to them. Do a little research on them to find out who they are and what their interests are.

2. **Make a positive impression:** If you want people to share their insights and resources, you need to get them to want to do it and help them remember to do it by:

    - **Have someone they respect introduce you:** If possible, do this. Referrals go a long way. Think about how much more you're open to with people that are introduced to you by someone you respect as opposed to a complete stranger.

- **Show your interest in them:** As previously stated, people are largely interested in themselves. They want your appreciation of their thoughts and activities. And they love people that are into what they are into. When meeting someone, show genuine interest in what they have done or said. Show them that you are interested in what they are interested in.

- **Try to help them achieve their goals:** Give first. You may not be able to give to someone but try your best to figure out a way to help them get what they want. Never expect anyone to help you simply because you want them to.

- **Be on point:** People like to be around awesome people. Be awesome; show up well-dressed and well-spoken. Smile and engage with others.

- **Show that you are serious or passionate:** Through conversation, show people that you have thought a lot about what you want to do and have acted to follow through. Don't detail your résumé, but share an experience that shows them you are serious. Tell your story.

- **Have something to give them:** Even with our best efforts, people tend to forget what is not in front of their eyes. Be creative and give them something to remember you by: a note, business card, token, or something.

3. **Let them know what you want to follow up about:** Whether it is to have lunch and get to know them better, share something with them, or inquire about how they can help, make it clear and get their approval.

4. **Get their contact info:** Ask them about the best way is to get in touch with them. Then, make sure you get that contact information.

5. **Follow up:** Where most people fail is following up. *Be sure to put it on your agenda to follow up with them.* Place reminders in your phone. Be persistent and don't give up. Some people are busy and need constant reminders. Follow up the day after, a week later, bi-weekly, then monthly depending on the relationship.

6. **Stay in contact:** Once you have established a relationship with someone, you want to maintain it. As a good rule of thumb, try to follow up with everyone in your network at least every six months. Depending on the nature of the relationship, you may have to do it more often. Start off with connecting with someone at least once a month. If the conversation is pressured or if there isn't anything to share, then make it at least every other month, then every three months, and so forth. This is how you get a sense of the person's schedule and personality enough to adjust accordingly.

Overall, being friendly to people and talking to them about how you may be able to assist with what they are doing opens many doors. Remember, people are interested in themselves. You have to connect with them on how you can help them. If you are strategic about your network, it will put you in the fast lane toward reaching your goals.

I am always networking. You never know what others may bring. For example, as I was nearing graduation, I was unsure about what exactly I was going to do after I received my degree. My goal was to teach for two years before going to graduate school. My ultimate teaching opportunity, which I purposefully set myself up for and EVERYONE thought I was going to get, rejected me. It was my first rejection and the biggest. I was crushed and confused. When I talked to one of my mentors about it, he was surprised but told me that he knew a principal of a local charter school that would be on campus next week at a book signing.

I attended the book signing with my résumé, business cards, and an elevator speech for the principal. As I made my way to him, some random man engaged me. I didn't want to be rude, so we began to converse. We had a wonderful conversation where I learned that students at his school had gone off to start schools and I shared with him about my passion to start a school. We connected and as the room started to clear, I realized that I needed to end the conversation, so I could speak with the principal. I asked for his card and he didn't have one, so I gave him mine and we parted ways on very good terms. However, the principal was gone. I was mad.

A few days later, I got an email from the man I was speaking to. He told me to stop by his school if I was ever in his area. When I scrolled down to his signature, I realized I was talking to the president of one of the top schools I was considering for grad school. It was shocking, to say the least! We continued to correspond, and he offered to bring me up to visit the school. I accepted. When I visited, he let me know about potential scholarships and offered to write the recommendation for acceptance into the school and the scholarships. It was very tempting, but I decided to work first before graduate school.

I share that story to show you how powerful networking can be. You never know who is in the room. If you know how to excel in human relations and are always prepared to network, doors will open for you.

Exercise P3.3 – Power Networking

Print business cards ASAP. Think about your goals and create a list of people who may be able to help you reach your goals. Create a list of people, locations, or events that can connect you with the people you need to meet. Follow the steps above to establish those connections.

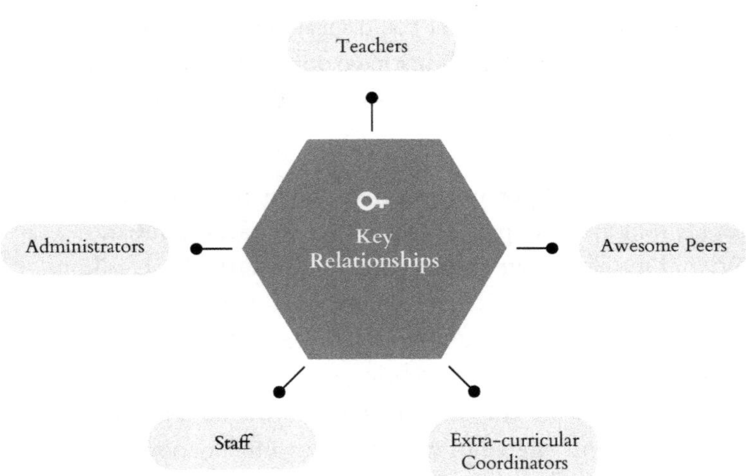

Building Strategic Relationships

In every environment you are in, there are going to be key players. People or groups of people that can be a significant influence on what you want to do in life. If you are going after a promotion, then that may be your boss or an HR representative. If you are in graduate school, that may be your advisor or any potential member of your dissertation committee. If you need money for school, that may be your teacher or a key person in the financial aid department. In every situation you are faced with, stay mindful of your goals and intentionally build relationships with the people who may be able to help you accomplish them.

In the school environment, there are four main groups of people you want to be intentional about making a good impression on:

- Leaders
- Teachers
- Staff
- Peers

Before we get into these, I want to re-emphasize that every opportunity I have taken advantage of has come from the relationships I've developed. Being very intentional about creating strong, meaningful connections and making a good impression on people will open you up to tons of opportunities.

Leaders

Every organization has a leadership structure. The leaders are usually the most knowledgeable and connected about what is going on in the organization. The president or principal of your school can give a strong recommendation to almost any person or opportunity within that institution and outside of it. Likewise, department heads, executives, and directors usually know the best people for you to connect with and the opportunities that are available. In every setting you are in, make it a point to ensure the leadership knows you, can speak highly about you, and think of you when they learn of opportunities.

The best way to connect with leaders is to do something extremely impressive for their organization. Win the highest award, accomplish something great, get people talking about you, lead an impressive event or workshop, do something that benefits and brings positive attention to their organization. Another way of getting that kind of a buzz going is to have someone they respect refer you to them.

Teachers

Teachers are critical to the academic setting. They are aware of so many opportunities and ways to improve your career, that it is ridiculous how many students overlook them. Remember, they have taught literally thousands of students just like you. They have taught many of the people in the careers you are probably interested in. They either know how to get there or can put you into contact with people those who have arrived.

Teachers have favorite students. They usually have a list of their best students. Many of them have kept in contact with those that have gone on to do some amazing things. They know which scholarships and awards these pupils have received and may have actually witten the necessary recommendations. They serve on selection committees and may have participated in the programs you are going after. Teachers know the information you are in school to get and have a treasure trove of insight on how you can take advantage of college. Above all else, they are the most important influence on your grade outside of your own effort.

As mentioned before, teachers are the gatekeepers. When they like you, they help you out. Therefore, you want to make an impression on them. If this is starting to sound like you are becoming someone you probably made fun of several years ago, understand that there is a way to go about everything. Show interest without seeming like a "kiss up." Your peers who have no real interest in getting the most out of college will never appreciate your mindset and that's fine; you'll need people to manage in the future.

First impressions last. Do you ever see the faculty or staff in pajamas or in clothes that should be reserved for only going out? No, because this is their job. Therefore, you want to be respectful of their work and act in a professional manner, too.

Teachers like to see students who:

- Arrive on time or early
- Are attentive and take notes
- Sit in the front of the class
- Are engaged and ask thoughtful questions

Creating relationships take time, but there are things you can do to put it in the fast lane. Here are 5 questions I asked all my teachers as soon as I could pull them aside. Usually, this was immediately after the first day of class or during their office hours. I adopted these from Dr. Joe Martin's book "*Tricks of the Grade*:"

1. How long have you been teaching this class?
2. Why this subject?
3. How can I get the most out of your class?
4. What does it take to get an A in this class?
5. What should I concentrate on to get an A in your class?

All these questions establish your interest in the teacher.

Continue to engage with your teacher. Pull them aside after class. Go to their office hours. Talk to them about the class and what you are doing in school. Share your opinions, and in the process, allow them to learn your story and who you are. Learn their story. Soon you will be comfortable about asking them if they know of any opportunities that would benefit you.

Having a great relationship with your teachers have many benefits: getting a better grade in the class, info about scholarships/programs, and letters of recommendations. Never take them for granted. Everyone has resources and insights that can be beneficial to you.

Staff

School is made up of two groups of workers: 1. Faculty, which are your professors and teachers and 2. Staff, your administrators, security guards, cafeteria staff, secretaries, etc.

Staff are one of the most overlooked groups of people, but they can be of tremendous assistance. All you must do is acknowledge them, be nice, and take a moment to get to know them. It is sad to see how many students or people in general overlook the humanity of staff. They are people, too. When you don't acknowledge them and continue to treat them like a bunch of low-class people who exist only to empty your trash or prepare your food, then you become just another random person to them. However, if you take a moment to engage with them in small talk, you can open doors to great possibilities. Let me give you a few personal scenarios:

- **Financial aid staff –** When I was in school, I made it a point to know the financial aid office staff. I visited my advisor regularly. I would stop by just to say hi on the premise that I was in the area. I would set an appointment and made up serious questions to ask. If I saw my advisor or financial aid staff around campus, I would engage with them in small talk. Every time I visited the office, I chatted it up with the secretary. When I had no money for one semester and needed to appeal to the director, I was able to get a highly coveted appointment almost immediately through my relationships with my financial aid advisor and the office secretary. That appointment led to over $13,000 in scholarships.
- **Security guards –** If I was ever in a rush, I could literally park wherever I wanted to, and the security guards would watch my car. No tickets, citations, or boots. If I wanted to get into an event, it was no problem. Now, tell me that ain't a benefit?!
- **Secretaries –** The most overlooked treasure trove in school. These are the people that know and work with the people you want to get to get to know. They

know what is going on in the department: scholarship opportunities, upcoming awards, events, gossip, etc. They usually know these things way before anyone else. If you get on their good side, you will be amazed at what they may give you the scoop on.

What I mean by acknowledging them is being nice, and getting to know them the same you would with a friend. If you walk by say "Hi!" Ask them how their day is. How's the family doing? What did they do over the weekend or break? I used to go a step further and get them stuff for holidays or find out what they liked and get it for them. I was just cool like that.

Some may call these things "manipulation," but making someone happy and, in return, having access to things that will make you happy makes the world a better place. If you approach all of this with the right spirit, people will respect you and gravitate toward you. I would much rather put a smile on someone's face and do something thoughtful for them, make moves among miserable people.

Peers

Do not overlook your classmates and those around you. Your peers are winning scholarships. They are in the top programs. They are doing things to ensure that their career is secured. They have successfully applied to opportunities. They have a wealth of resources. You will be amazed at where your peers will be later in life. If you develop good relationships with them, they can share countless insights that can help you with your career goals.

Also, make an effort to associate with the smart kids; the people you notice are on point. The saying, "Birds of a feather flock together," has more truth to it than you can imagine. The company you keep will either lift you up or bring you down. Be intentional about hanging around people who will challenge or inspire you to be better. Most importantly, be that person for those around you as well. **This is one of the most important pieces of advice in this book.** It will serve you well. Also, never discount where someone may be headed. I have friends all over the world who will give me a place to rest my head, legal advice, or the inside scoop on things others will never know.

EVERYTHING you do in society, and I mean EVERYTHING you do, will happen through interactions with people. People run the world. Being able to tap into that resource will lead to limitless possibilities.

Exercise P3.4 – Building Strategic Relationships

List leaders, teachers, staff, and peers who would be important to build a relationship with. Follow the suggestions above to establish those connections.

Getting Strong Recommendations

Strategically pick your recommenders

Be Awesome

Get them to adore you

Securing Strong Recommendations and References

When someone writes you a letter of recommendation or becomes a reference, they are vouching for you. Usually, writing a letter is much more significant because someone has taken the time to put on paper his or her impression of who you are and why you deserve to be selected. To secure a strong recommendation or reference, someone must have seen your work, attest to how good it is, and like you. These three factors are cultivated as you get your education and develop your experiences. Your recommendations and references will mainly come from teachers, supervisors, or colleagues you have interacted with during those times. To build a pool of people who can write strong recommendations and be great references, you must impress people as you get involved and take classes. Start early and be strategic about developing relationships with people who can give influential recommendations.

Once you have impressed people, there are three major factors you must consider when you select someone to refer you:

1. Who they are
2. What they can say about you
3. How passionate they are about their support for you

The Recommender

You always want to think carefully about who is recommending you and for what. References and recommendations should come from people who have direct experience with what you have done; usually this would be a supervisor. However, in some cases it may be more appropriate for someone who is aware of your activities and can attest to your performance. In every case, you need to be strategic in who you select to recommend you for something.

If you are going into business on Wall Street, you wouldn't want your art teacher as the main person writing a recommendation. Instead, you should aim for people who can emphasize the best qualities applicable to what you are applying to attain. For example, if you are applying to Harvard for college, you would probably want a professor from Harvard, or at least someone from an Ivy League institution for a recommendation. It would be even better if they taught in the field of your interest. If not, then the second person on your list for a recommendation should be in the area that you want to pursue. If you want to go to law school, you would want your recommendations to come from your English teacher, debate coach, or philosophy professor. Moreover, the more important the person giving the recommendation is within the hierarchy, the better. Should you get the adjunct professor to write you a recommendation or the dean of the department? Do you want your recommendation to come from your advisor or the president of the school?

As always, you want to be strategic about who you choose. This means that you are also strategic about who you have built relationships with, although it is a good rule to be cordial with everyone, when possible. Not everyone you build relationships with is meant to be a source for a recommendation letter. Different people have different strengths. If the reference or recommender cannot fulfill the other two factors, then don't even think of them as a choice.

Their Detail

Think about it: if you received a paragraph about someone that seems like a reiteration of a résumé, compared to a full-page letter detailing a story about someone else and what the recommender admired about them, who would you pick? More than likely, the detailed story. You would be amazed at how many people ask for recommendations from people that barely know them and what they do. If they don't know you, what you have done, or how well you have performed, then they are not a good choice to recommend you. You want to make sure your recommender can talk about you as person, not about your rrésumé. They should be able to give a detailed explanation of who you are *tailored to your strong suit as it relates to the application.*

This last point is key. You want to make sure your recommender or reference speaks to a specific quality, skill, or experience that is suited to what you are applying for. Just like your résumé and educational experience, your recommendation should be a custom fit for what you are applying for.

Their Passion

One of the things that many books don't emphasize, but makes a world of difference, is the passion the recommender expresses in recommending you. I had a professor that once told me there is a specific line that he only puts in his strongest recommendations, "without hesitation I wholeheartedly believe this student is capable of_____." You want your recommender to praise and advocate for you like they would for themselves. You want them to be able to write the strongest recommendation they have ever written for anyone.

The Steps to Obtaining Strong Recommendations

So how do you ensure you have strong recommendations?

- **Make sure your recommender knows & likes you –** Talk to them about your life and struggles and engage with them about their interests.
- **Shine in every interaction you have with them –** Excel in their presence. Earn those As. Do your best. Always be pleasant and professional.
- **Figure out who writes strong recommendations –** Some people write better than others. Some take writing letters of recommendations seriously and some will not. I have people who know me very well and would highly recommend me over the phone, but do not write strong letters of recommendations. This is something you will have to figure out by asking others or seeing the recommendation before they send it. Some say its taboo, but I ask for copies of my recommendations. I like to keep a portfolio with them.

Recommendations are evaluated on

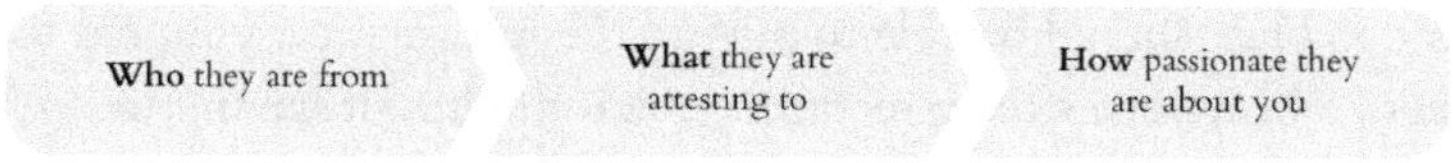

Who they are from → **What** they are attesting to → **How** passionate they are about you

Asking for someone to be a reference is much easier than for a letter of recommendation. With a reference, all you have to do is give them the heads up and let them know:

1. What you are applying for
2. Why you are applying
3. What you would like them to emphasize about you
4. When they should expect a call

When asking for a letter, you want to make sure your recommender has enough time to write the letter. At least two weeks in advance is standard. Ask them about it at least a month in advance of **your** two-week deadline. Even if you don't know the details of your application, let them know you are thinking about it. Now, this is very important: specifically ask them "can you write me a *strong* letter of recommendation?" If there is any hesitation, then you may not want them to write one for you. If they say yes, send them the following details:

- Description of what you are applying to
- List of things you would like them to emphasize (grade in their class, specific experience, skills, qualities, etc.)
- Timeframe/deadline (**should be at least two weeks before you want to submit the application**)
- How to submit the recommendation (online, sealed letter to you, sent directly to the entity)
- The essay you are submitting as part of the application.

You want to make it as easy as possible for them. Give them all the details they need and limit any guesswork they would have to do. They should be able to pull up the information you sent to them and write a strong recommendation without having to do anything extra.

The best way to make it easy to get a strong recommendation is to ask if they would like you to develop the first draft. If they say yes, put yourself in their shoes and write the best recommendation they could possibly create. Do not include anything they could not say themselves through their interaction with you.

Also, always have at least 1-2 more people for recommendation letters than you need just in case someone doesn't submit it on time or can't do it. Ask them if you can have a copy for your personal portfolio. Some recommenders don't want you to see their recommendations. Those that will allow it, please do. If you can see the recommendation before it is sent, you can judge whether it fits your application package. Remember you are submitting a package. You want to make sure everything paints a picture of who you are.

Be sure to thank them. A handwritten note or a card goes a long way.

Exercise P3.5 – Securing Strong Recommendations and References

Identify people who would be strong recommenders and references for your career goals. Review your list of Who's Who. Once they are identified, be intentional about applying the tips in this chapter to build a strong relationship.

Remember:

- Relationships are hands down, the most important pillar of *The Academic Hustle*. The majority of career development opportunities are secured based upon the strength of relationships.
- Be intentional about excelling in human relations. Cultivate the qualities of being good person. As we all know, one of the best recommendations any one can give is "She/He is a good person."
- Being able to converse pleasantly with someone is one of the most important factors in developing meaningful relationships.
- The saying, "your network is your net worth," is real. Building genuine connections with people will take you far.
- There are people in the academic environment that you should make sure you build relationships with. Be strategic.
- All recommendations are not equal. You want to make sure you secure strong recommendations for the opportunities you are going after.

Pillar #4: Tailor Your Presentation

Different strokes for different folk.
—Sly & The Family Stone

In this section you will learn to:

- Present yourself as the best candidate for each opportunity you apply to.
- Do research on opportunities.
- Always be ready to secure an opportunity on the spot.
- Crafting impressive cover letters, essay responses, and personal statements.

I abhorred the idea of suits. I am from Miami, Florida. It gets hot. I could not understand why someone would put on so many layers of clothes in such heat, and then put a noose (tie) around their neck just to look "professional." It just did not make sense to me.

Like most kids growing up, I took pride in being me. How I dressed, how I spoke, and how I acted was me being me. Why should I change myself for someone else or for "society?" My sagging pants were an indication of where I was from. My hair was in locs. I did not believe in always having to "keep it up" either. It was my hair. It was ME. It should grow naturally. I had issues with addressing people as well. That part of the deal always had mixed cues. I did not like to look strangers straight in the eyes because doing so was either disrespectful or called for a challenge. I spoke a dialect of English some would call "Ebonics" or "slang." That was just how I talked. Why should I change that? If I did not know you, why should I "get to know you?" If you looked a certain way or spoke a certain way, I did not like you anyway. What do I care if you do not like me, or if I offended you, with your sensitive self? I was not trying to be your friend. I did not need any new friends. My experience at Morehouse completely changed that mentality.

It was the norm on campus to dress in professional attire. I witnessed students who were well-dressed and well-spoken be received by faculty and staff with the respect that I craved. Even though I was a top student and had a more extensive résumé, these suited up students were welcomed with smiles. I had to work four times as hard for people to overlook how I presented myself. I would watch and overhear a student speak with a professor, and they would recommend opportunities that the student could take advantage of; when I walked into the office, I could not get them to tell me about the exact same opportunity without directly asking them about it. I cannot count how many times other students were given the VIP treatment over me, even though, on paper, I was "better."

At first it angered me. I thought I was being discriminated against. Prejudged. Treated unfairly. Dismissed because I was from Miami. I rebelled against it by becoming even more awesome, forcing them to recognize me. On a positive note, that motivated me to become a high-achiever. Yet, on the other hand, I was rebelling against a fundamental law: People are human. People like what they like. People open up to others that look and talk like them.

How you present yourself is very important. When you are in a professional environment, there will always be a dress code, a certain etiquette, a decorum. Once you know the standard, you can choose whether to meet or exceed it. Operating below or outside of the standard will indefinitely hinder your goals. Meeting or exceeding the standard will make the path to your goals much easier.

All the other components prepare you for this one. Your education, experience, and relationships teach you the language of your career, provide you with opportunities to experience, and give you constant feedback. By excelling in each of the previous three pillars, you can develop all that it takes to present yourself as the ideal candidate. This section sets you up to do so, which is possible *when you* understand what they want.

Getting jobs, scholarships, and taking advantage of other opportunities is not about you. It is about them, what they want, and whether you are a good fit for them. To succeed, you must give them what they want. That starts with identifying what they are after. To do that, you must do your research.

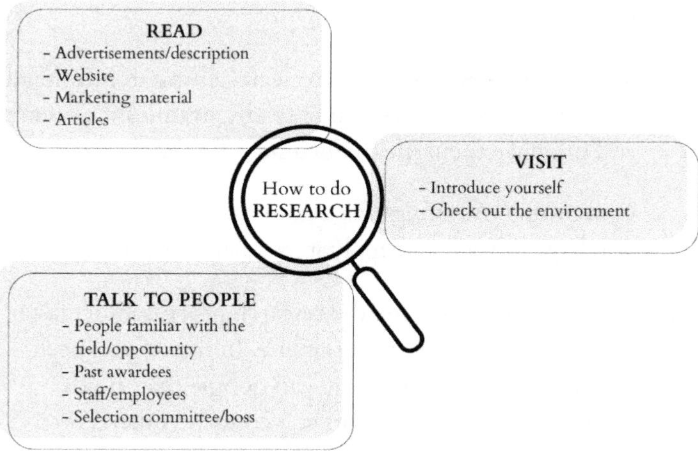

How to Research Opportunities

Researching is a basic skill in life that must be mastered if you plan to move up in the world. Research helps you understand the full scope of something. What are people saying about it? What is its current state? What information is there about the subject? What are the facts? Basically, research helps you understand what is going on at a deeper level. It is a tool for understanding and fact checking.

Research is a pretty simple process that involves five basic steps:

1. **Know what you want –** The first step, as in all things, is to identify your topic and/or your question. For us, we want to know about the company, scholarship, or program we are applying to.

2. **Read –** Depending on what you are researching, you will look through websites, articles, periodicals, and books to understand your topic.

3. **Talk to people –** This comes after reading because you want to get a basic understanding of the topic, so that you can ask the right questions without sounding clueless when talking to someone.

4. **Take notes –** As you begin to search through information, you want to make sure you note any significant elements and organize them into a document for quick review.

5. **Conclude –** All things must come to an end. Review what you have learned and apply it to what you need to do.

Modern technology has made the research process much faster. You can find just about anything online. In fact, if you need to know "how to do research" you can google that. If you want to know about recent events at a company, then enter the "company name" and "news" into a search engine. If you want to find out the top schools for your profession, look up "your profession's name" and "top schools." The possibilities are endless. Use the technology at your fingertips to prepare you for your presentation.

When it comes to applying for something, the focus of your research should be on identifying what they the company, school, non-profit, scholarship committee, etc. wants.

Identify What They Want

To identify what a selection committee wants, you need to understand who they are. To understand who they are, you need to look at what they say about themselves, what they have accomplished, and what others have said about them. As you get to know the entity, focus on identifying exactly what it is that they want for the opportunity you are applying to. This can be found by reviewing an institution's:

- History
- Mission
- Vision
- Values
- Leadership team
- Recent news and accomplishments
- What others have said about them (reputation)
- Eligibility requirements
- Selection criteria
- Selection committee participants
- Past awardees

You want to get as much information about them as possible within the timeframe you have. You can do this by:

- Reviewing their website and any of their publication materials
- Doing an online search
- Asking people within their office
- Speaking to anyone you know who knows about them
- Talking to anyone who has been accepted or awarded from their organization
- Looking at similar opportunities and institutions

The purpose of this exercise is to collect as much information as you can about who they are to figure out what it is they want. While doing this, pay close attention to how they describe themselves, what they focus on, and the language they use.

What you are looking for makes up the characteristics of the entity. The repeated key words are what make them different from everyone else. This is their **language**. These are the things that will show you what they want. For example, let's look at the mission of two major technology companies:

Apple - *"Apple designs Macs, the best personal computers in the world, along with OS X, iLife, iWork and professional software. Apple leads the digital music revolution with its iPods and iTunes online store. Apple has reinvented the mobile phone with its revolutionary iPhone and App Store and is defining the future of mobile media and computing devices with iPad."*

As you can see from reading this, Apple is focused on designing excellent products at the very cutting-edge of society. They want to be leaders and pioneers in their field. Based upon Apple's language, you would focus your presentation on leadership and innovation with actual work done.

Microsoft – *"Our mission is to empower every person and every organization on the planet to achieve more."*

Microsoft's language is about the worldwide development of people. If you are engaging with Microsoft, then your language should be centered on how you can improve and empower people and organizations. You want to emphasize your desire to assist people in accomplishing more.

It is that simple: speak people's language through your experiences.

The most important piece of information to concentrate on is the past awardees or the type of people they have accepted in the past. All those people were accepted for a reason. Being able to find out why those people were accepted and then model what they did is a proven way to seal the deal.

The earlier you can get this information the better. That is why it is important to know what you want. If you ultimately wanted to work for Google in their product development department under the Vice President of Innovation, you can do your research to identify the education that is most appealing to them, the experience that will make you a strong candidate, build the relationships that can connect you to the right people, and tailor your application and personal story to the desires of the person you want to work under. This may take a few years to do, but it will create a very strong application. This same method can be applied to getting into graduate school, which emphasizes working under a specific professor. Someone who knows their end goal and follows the process to realize it will have a much greater chance of getting accepted than someone who applies to everything and does not tailor their application.

If you do your research and identify what they want, all you have to do is give that to them.

Exercise P4.1 – Identifying Their Language

Select two businesses or non-profits in the same field. Review their websites and note the descriptive adjectives they use to describe themselves and what they care about. Compare and contrast the companies. How are they different? Select an applicable experience from your résumé and describe the experience in two different ways using the language of each company.

Presenting Yourself as the Ideal Candidate

When applying, your goal is to present yourself as the ideal candidate. Through research, you get an idea of what that candidate looks like. As people, we put a heavy emphasis on how things are presented. If it looks good, sounds good, smells good, tastes good, and/or feels good, then we are tempted to try it. Therefore, your presentation is crucial. The other pillars give you the insight, experience, and exposure to present yourself well. If you do not excel at this component, then you are going to have some hard time securing opportunities. On the other hand, if you do this step extremely well, then you can get yourself into almost any door. However, if you don't have the substance built by the other components, you will ultimately fail as you walk through that door.

There are some key factors to ensure that you present yourself well in every environment:

1. **Preparation –** The first step to making sure that you present yourself well is to know how the ideal person would present themselves in the same circumstance. Be clear on what they want and take the time to practice presenting yourself as that person.

2. **Appearance –** How you look is VERY important. Being clean and dressing with a confident style opens countless doors. Let's face it, people judge books by their cover. There is no getting around it. Make your cover spectacular. Invest in clothes that look amazing on you. On the other hand, what you submit reflects who you are. Put time into making everything you give to someone look as amazing as possible. Your research into the opportunity should inform you on how to ensure what you present is received well. Looking good will show them how you, in turn, will make them look good.

3. **Communication –** Your presentation (verbal and non-verbal) should communicate a clear and confident image of who you are and what you can do. Your belief in yourself will inspire other's confidence in you. A firm handshake and eye contact is important. Your preparation should be so solid that you'll be ready for whatever may come your way. You want to talk to people with the level confidence and comfort you would have speaking to your friend about your favorite subject.

On the Spot

Being ready for an on the spot evaluation of who you are and what you can bring to the table opens quite a few doors. You never know whom you may meet randomly or to whom people are connected to. You may not be in front of the decision-maker, but you may be in front of the person who can get you there. Learning how to impress someone on the spot can be helpful at networking events, and college or career fairs. Rest assured, it's easier than you think. To impress someone on the spot there are two things you need to have:

1. Talking Points
2. Something to give

Talking Points: As you prepare for all environments it would be a good idea to have a few talking points. These are concepts, facts, or understandings about a topic. They can be used to start or continue a conversation. You can also develop a brief elevator speech about topics important to you and your profession. The point of having talking points is to be able to communicate to people your competence. Also, they are perfect to introduce ideas and interests.

Talking points are helpful in almost all environments. Before going to a family gathering or hanging out with friends, there may be a few stories or jokes you want to tell. If you are attending an event or conference, have a few ideas about the topic or craft a few while you're there to discuss with others. This is not to make you come off as robotic and calculated, but to help you be comfortable in what can become second nature. Having some things prepared to say helps you break the ice for people to be open with you. Eventually, as you intentionally develop talking points for different environments, you will, over time, become a world-class person.

Exercise P4.4 – Developing Talking Points

Think about the next person you are going to talk to or the next environment where you will engage people. Do a little research and develop talking points to engage someone in a 3-5 minutes conversation.

One of the most common ways to package your talking points and introduce yourself is with an elevator conversation. As you prepare for a networking event and/or college/career fair, it will be important for you to have an elevator conversation ready.

Elevator Conversation

People do not like to be pitched. They like to be engaged. After all, we are inundated with advertisements. Imagine a telemarketer pestering you on the phone, manipulating you it seems, into staying on the line to agree to something you have no interest in at all. There is a natural mental bracing when we hear someone giving us a speech. They have their opinions and desires. All of which have no importance in our mind – unless they are giving us what we want.

While in school, I attended quite a few career development workshops. One of the techniques almost always emphasized was the elevator speech. An **elevator speech** is a quick 30 second to 2-minute talk that you can give at the drop of a dime to introduce yourself, your product, or your services to someone. The name comes from the idea of meeting someone important in an elevator and grabbing their interest while succinctly introducing yourself before they get off.

Here's another opportunity to learn from my mistakes. I was told to craft an elevator speech to be used at career fairs and networking events. I did. It went like this:

> Hi, my name is Matthew Pigatt. I am a Psychology and African American studies major at Morehouse College. I am involved in quite a few things on and off-campus: I am President of the William Tucker Society – The African American Studies Club, Vice President of the AUC's Association of Black Psychologists club and I conduct research through NIMH-COR Honors Undergraduate Research Training Program and the UNCF/Mellon Mays Undergraduate Fellowship. My goal is to become a professor but before I go to graduate school, I want to teach 9th grade high school after I graduate.

Saying the same thing repeatedly to almost everyone I met at networking events and career fairs produced the same response repeatedly. Just as I was about to list all the things I was involved in (this was the only part that changed), I would notice people's eyes start to glaze over. They were not interested at all in all the things I was doing. I noticed quite a few people becoming annoyed. I became annoyed too. Who wants to hear some random person bragging about themselves? Not me.

So, I decided to engage the people I wanted to connect with in conversation. I would go up to a recruiter and ask them questions about who they were representing or at networking events I would ask people what brought them to the event and what they did. It was better than the elevator speech because it got people talking. Those that were not talkative would end the conversation almost immediately after answering my questions. Those that were talkative would elaborate instead of just answering the question. Almost all the conversations had no depth to them. That felt better than spouting off that dry list of my accomplishments, but I soon got bored, yet again. I did not like just talking to random people for the sole purpose of getting something from them.

I began to think: how can I engage people? How can I get them to open up to me quickly? How can I connect with them and not feel as though I am using them? How can I make a real connection with someone? That began the process of developing what I call the elevator conversation.

Building rapport was something I became good at. It was common for me to meet someone and quickly engage them in conversation about their interests. I always left these conversations feeling good. Moreover, the people I would connect with remembered me and almost always took the time out to talk. I wondered how to apply building rapport with the people I met at networking and career fairs.

I knew I had to introduce myself, but I also had to get the other person to open up. The social scientist in me began to experiment. After months of trying different approaches and reflecting on what worked and what didn't, the following emerged.

First, before beginning you must…you guessed it…prepare and do your research!

- Know the organization, company or individual. If you are attending an event, be sure to learn about who is hosting the event and the history of the event
- Understand the nature of the event. What is the format? Is it a meet and greet? Will there be on the spot interviews?
- Know who will be there and what they have to offer
- Select 3-5 people you want to target and thoroughly research them using the points we discussed above

These items help you figure out what you want from the event, give you talking points as you interact with people, and a clear idea of what you should emphasize in your elevator conversation.

For the event I spoke about earlier where I met the college president, my preparation was simple. The event was a book launch for a professor I knew well. His book was on leadership. I found out that there would be a meet and greet, then a panel discussion, and that a well-known school chancellor was expected to be in attendance. My goal was to connect with the charter school chancellor to get a job as a teacher. Therefore, I had my *tailored* résumé ready, and I crafted my elevator conversation for the chancellor:

> Hi, my name is Matthew Pigatt. Mr. Keno Sadler told me to make sure I connected with you. I am graduating magna cum laude in May with degrees in Psychology and African American studies. My dream is to start a high school that prepares students for college and career success. I have spent the last three years in some of the top programs in the country conducting national award-winning research on people who have overcome the odds and became high-achievers in school and their career. I have been sharing my research while tutoring and conducting workshops for kids in local schools for years. I would love to take it to another level and teach them. Mr. Sadler told me that your school would be a great place for me to develop my work. [I made a comment about his school from the research I did but forgot what it was…oops]. Could you tell me what makes your school different from the rest?

A speech like this can be used to approach anyone about a job and is very useful during a career fair. If you look closely there are a few elements:

- **My name –** It amazes me how many people don't say their names clearly. Make it a point to say it.
- **Person who referred me –** As mentioned earlier, people are more open to individuals that have been confirmed by others. If you know someone connected to the person or organization, be sure to mention their name at the beginning.
- **Credentials –** You are talking to the person in hopes of getting a job. Briefly mention your experience and certifications.

- **Goals –** Sharing your goals helps a person put what you are doing into perspective. It lets them know how their work fits into your "master plan." This is significant to employers because it shows that you are not just trying to get another dollar from them.
- **Why you want the job –** Doing this gives them a better understanding of what drives you; what would motivate you to do a great job.
- **Achievements –** Remember, people like success. They would like to know that you are accomplished. Share a significant achievement.
- **Insightful comment about the entity –** This lets them know you have done your research—the mark of a prepared person.
- **Thoughtful question –** People like to talk. Give them the opportunity to do it. Ask a question that gets them to share their opinion. Try not to ask a question that gets them repeating the same old talking points they give to everyone that asks them the obvious fact-based questions.

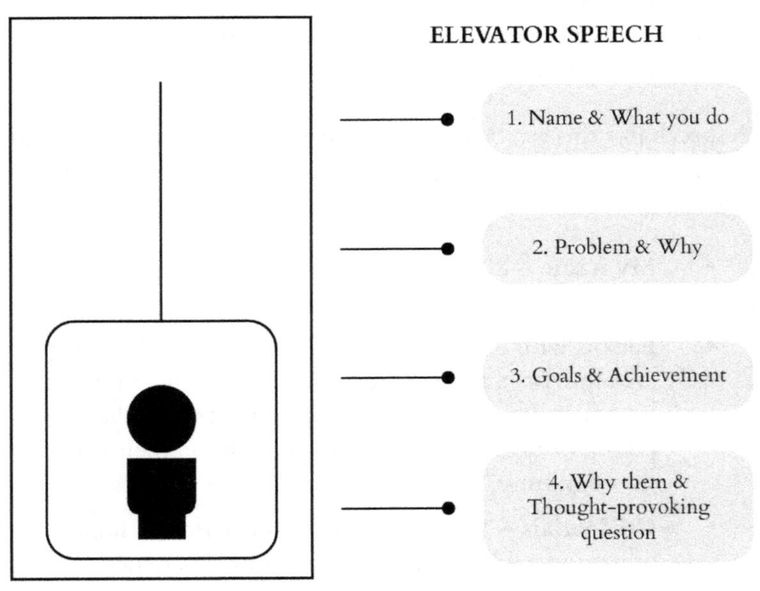

If you are speaking to a person one-on-one, your elevator conversation should be no more than 60 seconds. If it is to a few people, then you can push it to two minutes. Lean toward keeping it as concise as possible while hitting the major points. If you know you are going to have more than a few minutes with a person, I would recommend breaking it down into talking points you could spread throughout the conversation. It is always better to ask thoughtful questions, to get the person talking, and make your points while responding to the conversation. That makes it more natural and personable.

When at a career fair or talking to someone specifically about a job, there are a couple key questions to ask:

- What does the ideal candidate for this position look like?
- What type of education? Experience? Qualities? Or skills will they have?

When they answer your questions, take notes, and start to think about what experiences you can share that fit this criterion. Briefly and excitedly, share those experiences using their language and then ask:

- If I were to apply to this position, what would you suggest I do to submit a strong application?

In reading this, some people may think this is too forward, but you will be surprised at what people will share to someone who has done the above. It is similar to the questions asked to the teacher at the beginning of class. Make sure you take note of their answer to this question and do what they say.

Lastly, be sure to get their contact information and ask for a good time to follow up with them. I spoke about the importance of having a business card earlier. That is part of following up to make sure you stay in their mind. People tend to forget what is not right in front of their face.

If you remember the story, you know I never got a chance to give that practiced speech to the school chancellor. A college president intercepted me. However, being that I was a graduating senior and had to make sure I was ready for all opportunities, I had already had an elevator conversation prepared for random occurrences. When this random man engaged me, I immediately adapted my standard elevator conversation to him:

> Hi, my name is Matthew Pigatt. My dream is to have a high school that prepares students for college and career success. These days all schools say they are preparing students for the next step, but very few emphasize having a post-secondary plan. Most will only focus on testing and graduating students. I was one of those kids that was going down the wrong path and didn't have a plan for my career development. Thankfully, I have been blessed with the opportunity to conduct national award winning research on high-achievers in school and the professional world. I want to empower others to also live out their dreams and become high-achievers. As a senior here at Morehouse, I am finishing up a degree in psychology, which helped me understand people. My other major in African American studies gives me a unique perspective into that group, which is where I would like to concentrate my energies. Dr. Walter Fluker is a mentor of mine and I am excited about his upcoming book. What brings you to this event?"

Of course, I did not just throw all of that out at him like a block of cheese. I would say a few lines and let him respond however he felt. Then, when the moment seemed right and natural, I added the next line or two. It was good that I prepared and mentioned my dream of opening a school because that is what got us engaged in a deep, easy-flowing conversation. He talked about how students at his school continued to go off and open schools. At the time, I didn't know he was a college president and a person who could open doors to great opportunities. He wasn't an unfortunate professional being jammed up and stressed out by some desperate kid. No, we were just two people connecting on similar interests. Nevertheless, I'm sure you noticed a couple key things I mentioned in this **standard elevator conversation:**

- **My name –** Don't forget to let them know your name.
- **What do I do –** This is standard. People like to know what a person does.
- **The problem I want to address –** This stimulates conversation and brings them into your world. It also lets them know what you can do specifically for them.
- **Why I am interested in this –** Give them the story. The reasoning. People like to know why and what makes someone tick.
- **My goals –** This can get them thinking about how they may be able to help.
- **An achievement –** Your achievement proves you're the real deal and separates you from the amateurs. Remember, people are drawn to those that achieve and make things happen.
- **My credentials –** Let people know that you have certifications behind you.
- **Why I am here at this moment –** This touches on commonality. What brought you both to this moment and place.
- **A question to get them talking –** If you do the above in the right way, then there should be a couple of items someone can engage you on. If they don't react or you have something you want to learn about them, simply ask a question to get them talking.

When at an event, conference, or another type of networking opportunity, these are good points to cover. Elevator conversations can be used in a variety of ways and have many elements. Most people use it to pitch their business. However, you can adapt it to almost all situations. When it comes to *The Academic Hustle,* it is used to introduce yourself to people who are connected to career development opportunities for you.

When I prepared my lil brother for a **college fair** this was his speech:

> Hi, my name is Randon Campbell. I am a senior at Miramar High School with a 4.3 GPA. I want to get into a college that can prepare me for my dream of becoming a dentist. I want to make sure I can stay active outside of class too. I currently serve as tuba section leader in the band and a few other things as well. I've looked through your material and am interested in your school because of *[insert something you are genuinely excited about (social life, specific degree, faculty, alumni, etc.)]*. Would you tell me more about [*insert what you want to learn more about (a specific degree program, extracurricular activities, why they* **personally** *believe the college is a good fit for them, what they* **personally** *believe makes the college different from others, or anything else that can get them talking about what they offer or want*?)]

He briefly introduced himself and immediately got them talking about what they want. From there, he asked the following question:

- Could you describe the student that would get accepted to your institutions on a full-ride scholarship?

He took notes and started to think about what experiences he could share that would fit with what they said. Briefly and excitedly, he shared those experiences using their language and then asked:

- If I wanted to submit my application with the possibility of getting a full-ride scholarship, what would be my next steps?

He wrote those things down. Thanked them. Gave him his portfolio and briefly reviewed it with them. Then he got their contact information to follow up.

If you present yourself in this manner you will stand out from the crowd that:

1. Don't attend these events.

2. Don't talk to the recruiters.

3. Just grab information or items from tables.

4. When they do approach, ask questions that are already covered in the material on the table or on their website.

5. Don't introduce themselves and their desires.

6. Don't ask for information on how to get accepted or scholarships.

7. Don't provide anything to remember them by.

8. Don't get their contact information.

Here are some final key items to make sure you have an engaging elevator conversation:

1. **Adapt to the person –** All people are human. We all have our likes and dislikes. The same elevator conversation will not work on everyone. It must be adapted to the circumstance and the person. Remember, this is about giving them what they want. Do your research, identify what they want, and use their language.

2. **Practice –** Practice makes perfect. Before an event or speaking with someone, I would repeat my elevator conversation out loud repeatedly. If I had time, I would write it out. If I didn't have time or was in a public place, I would quickly write down a few key points and craft the speech in my head. Then I would run through it over and over in my head until I had it down. The result was almost always an impressive introduction. As they say, "first impressions matter."

3. **Refine** – As with all things, we can't be stagnant; using the same approach verbatim will get old. Different situations will require, at the very least, small variations. That's a good thing because it keeps you on your toes. Be sure to observe how people react to your speech overall and to specific parts. Use that knowledge to keep certain parts, strengthen others, and include information that people want to hear. Based upon how people react and the questions they ask after it, you can continue to create an even more impressive speech. The more people you do it in front of and the more you adapt it to them, the better it will get.

Exercise P4.5 – Developing an Elevator Conversation

Using the information above develop the following:

1. A 30-second introduction of yourself with one question for a person
2. A 60-second introduction of yourself and what you are looking for with one question for a person
3. A 60-second introduction of yourself, what you are looking for, and something interesting about who you are engaging, tailored to a specific environment, person or opportunity with 3-5 questions

Now as I mentioned before, people tend to forget most of what someone say almost immediately after speaking with them. That is why it is important to have something to give the person to jog their memory. That's where a portfolio comes into play. But, first let's build on this idea of crafting your presentation when interviewing.

Interviewing to Win

Interviews are a matter of confidence. Confidence in your capacity to fulfill the role you are applying to and being able to get the interviewer(s) to feel confident that you can be a part of their team. As with essays, there are plenty of books and articles online with valuable advice on how to have excellent interviews. I would strongly encourage you use them while preparing and practicing for your interviews.

There are a few ways to ensure you have the confidence in your capacity to fulfill the role you are applying to:

1. Go after positions where you know you will do whatever it takes to excel in because you either enjoy it, it would set you up for something else, or you have another powerful reason to succeed.

2. Plan ahead and strategically develop the education and experiences that will prepare you for the role.

3. Learn everything you can about the wants and needs of the organization and the position you are applying to.

As you may have guessed, this strategy is not for people who apply to anything and everything with the hopes of just getting a job. That is one of the worst ways to go after a job. However, being strategic and going after things that will build upon your talents and interest and develop your career will give you the confidence you need to have an excellent interview.

Once you are fully confident in your capacity to fulfill the role you are applying to, you must be able to communicate that confidence to your interviewer in a way that will encourage them to believe in your ability to be a part of their team. Here are a few things you can do to communicate that confidence:

1. Prepare and practice answering the most common interview questions using their language to tell stories that describe your experience.

2. Create a 1-2-page cheat sheet about the company and interviewer(s) using the points discussed above and review it before walking into the interview.

3. Before and during the interview, repeat to yourself all the reasons why you KNOW you are the best candidate for the job.

4. During the interview, be very professional, but build rapport and act like you are talking to a new friend.

5. Express your passion and seriousness about doing this job well through the stories you tell of your experiences.

If you set yourself up in the right way, the interview can be more of a formality. Almost all the jobs I have interviewed for have been like this. What I mean, is that you can already be hired before you get to the interview. Walking into an interview knowing you already have the job and talking to the interviewer(s) as if you are sharing with your future colleagues why you are going to work well with them is a serious confidence boost. Making this happen is all about relationships.

If you want to set yourself up with a job before the interview, you must provide a very strong recommendation to the person making the hiring decision. People don't like to think much. If they receive a strong recommendation from someone they trust about a decision, then they will most likely go with the endorsement. This is where your network and performance while gaining your education and experience come into play. If you have impressed your professors, got involved in an array of activities in your field, created lasting relationships, and shined brightly in all areas, then you will have a strong network. When looking for a job, either express what you desire to your network and ask them if they can recommend you to anything or find an opportunity and ask someone in your network who has close ties to the decision-maker to personally recommend you. This is how I got my internship and job after graduation, and almost all the opportunities I have received. The deal was basically sealed before I got there. All I had to do was present myself well.

Make it a point to prioritize how you present yourself. Use online information and as many resources as you can to strengthen your skills in building rapport, communication, essay writing, and interviewing. Your presentation is one of the most important factors to submitting award-winning applications.

As human beings, we have a bias about how things are presented. Looks and appearances will get someone in the door. Therefore, anything you do to improve how you present yourself will at least get you a meeting. However, your education, experience, relationships, and determination to excel will ensure that you are a competitive candidate to the opportunities you pursue.

Exercise P4.3 – Impressive Interviewing

Conduct an online search for the "top interview questions." Select 10 questions that are not job specific. Using Exercise P4.1, craft responses that incorporate your research of each company.

Cover Letters, Essay Questions, & Personal Statements

Your cover letters, essay question responses, or personal statements are usually the selection committee's first impression of you. In most applications, the point of this section is to see what you have to say about yourself. They have your education and experience on paper, as well as what someone else says about you. Now, they want to know what you have to say about yourself. They want to get to know you and your reasoning for who you are and why you want to join them. That is what you must give them. No matter what the question or format is, you must put your story, your why and your desires into whatever you write for an application. The clearer and more articulate you are, the better.

The main point I want to make on this topic is to ensure that anything you submit in writing is tailored to whatever you are applying for. Every sentence is an opportunity to show the specific selection committee exactly why you are the best candidate. It is very important that you speak directly to the specific selection committee and not use the same answer or essay used for another opportunity. As I alluded to (and outright stated) earlier, your complete package, including your essay, should be tailored specifically to the opportunity you are applying for. You should use their language and address it to the people who will be reviewing your application.

There are a couple of things you want to keep in mind:

1. Before you start writing, conduct an online search for "how to write great cover letters/essays/personal statements." Select two to three articles and use them as guides as you write.

2. Capture your audience with an attention-grabbing opener.

3. Follow an outline that clearly states your main point and the supporting details.

4. Be you. Talk about your passions and why you do what you do.

5. Write like you are speaking directly to the person who is providing you with the opportunity.

6. Show don't tell. Use stories to describe your experience, qualities, and skills. Don't reiterate your résumé. Your writing should complement your package.

7. Close with how their opportunity will build you as a person and help you reach your goals.
8. Take at least 3 days to write and rewrite.
9. Proofread and get others, especially those that are familiar with the opportunity, to review and edit it.

When it comes to cover letters:

- Be concise. Read over what you wrote multiple times and try your best to cut out everything that isn't directly relevant. Feel free to use bullet points where appropriate.

For essay questions:

- Be sure to answer the question completely. Read over the question and make sure you can clearly point to where you address every aspect of the question in your answer.

While writing personal statements:

- You can mention your struggles but spend the majority of your essay illustrating the story of how you overcame them to become the ideal candidate.
- Your emphasis should be on your area of interest, followed by the how and why you became interested.

Your writing should display that you were made for the opportunity. Everything in your life prepared you for them. When both of you come together, there will be a win-win situation that brings forth growth, collaboration, and awesomeness. If you don't get that feeling after reading what you wrote, rewrite, and continue to edit. Keep doing that until you and everyone who reads it has that feeling.

I'm not a very good writer, but I'm an excellent rewriter.
—**James Michener**

Throw away the idea that you are going to write the perfect sentence or essay on your first try. This isn't a movie. That RARELY happens. The best writers write, rewrite, edit, proofread, rewrite, proofread, edit, proofread, and on and on and on. Take your time with it.

If you use multiple articles or books as evaluation criteria for your writings, tailoring your answers to the specific opportunity, and follow the points above, you should craft award-winning essays.

Exercise P4.2 – Writing Excellence

Conduct an online search for at least 3 – 5 articles/ examples that address each of the following:

- How to write a great cover letter
- Best college essays
- Writing excellent personal essays

Using the information learned from these articles, create a checklist of the things you must do to improve your writing for each of these.

Develop a Working Portfolio

The elevator conversation is part of making a memorable impression. People will forget what you said. Giving them something that reminds them of who you are and what you are about will make your impression last. What you give is based upon the environment you are in.

If you are at a networking event, then a business card is usually the best way to go. If your business card doesn't speak to what you presented to them, then write a couple key points of what you said on the back of it. The point is to give them something to jog their memory of you.

If you are looking for a job, then you need to have your résumé and cover letter on hand always. You would need them if you were putting in an application, so have them ready to give directly to a person who can either make the decision whether to hire you, or can forward them to the person that can. It is always best to submit your application directly to the person with decision-making authority. As stated before, your résumé and cover letter should be tailored to the opportunities of that position. Putting in a letter of reference or two would make you even more of a stand out.

When attending a career fair, I would find out the specific companies I wanted to approach and develop a résumé and cover letter specifically for those companies. If I only knew the industry, then I would develop a general cover letter and résumé tailored to that industry.

Do your research and look at job descriptions for the potential positions you are going after. That can help you tailor your material.

If you are approaching someone about a scholarship, internship, program, or fellowship, then having a tailored cover letter, résumé, recommendation letters, and work examples on hand would be impressive to whomever you are talking to.

When attending a college fair or pursuing scholarship opportunities, the same method would apply. Do your research and put together a few tailored portfolios with the following items:

1. Cover letter
2. Résumé
3. Recommendation letters

4. Work examples

Cover Letter

Cover letters are used as quick summaries of what you want and why you deserve it. You want one of these as the first page of your portfolio so that someone could quickly understand what you are giving them and why. If you are creating a portfolio for a specific opportunity, you will tailor it to the specific person, organization, and prospect. Remember, if you do not have a specific opportunity in mind, tailor it to the industry, organization, and/or department as much as possible. You can use the cover letter format in emails you send to people, too. Keep in mind the following when drafting a cover letter:

- Use a standard template found online.
- Address it to a specific person. If you do not have a specific person, use "To whom it may concern."
- First paragraph discusses why you are writing the letter, what you want, and why you want it.
- Second paragraph discusses what makes you the ideal candidate.
- Have a bullet list of what is in the portfolio.
- Last paragraph should briefly address any negative areas in your application in a positive way.

Tailored Résumé

All résumés should be tailored to specific opportunities. To save time on having to reinvent yourself for every job opportunity, simply tweak your master résumé/CV. Once an opportunity presents itself, just find a résumé template for that specific field. Yes, I put a 'just' in that statement; it's not as difficult as you think. For example, if you were applying to a research job at an academic university you would conduct an online search for résumés of that type and modify one that fits you. Next, you would identify active verbs for that field. These can be found by reviewing the résumé you came across in the last step and researching the field. Words like synthesized, researched, collected, conducted, analyzed, are examples for an academic research job. Finally, select appropriate experiences from your master résumé and modify the language you used to describe the experience to align with the language of the opportunity. Keep the following in mind:

- Maintain a uniform standard format that is clear and easy to scan and identify important information.
- Write one to two sentences describing the job and type of work for your position.
- Create a bullet point list starting with active verbs of the industry describing what you accomplished while at the job.
- Quantify your accomplishments with numbers as much as possible.

Recommendation Letters

Recommendation letters are an essential component of a portfolio. People like to see what other people say about you. Include at least two to five letters in your portfolio. Make it a habit of securing strong recommendation letters for every major experience in your master résumé. Ideally, letters should be on an official letterhead and signed by the recommender.

Work Examples

Let your work speak for itself. Include copies of test scores, transcripts, writing samples, awards, certificates, pictures, designs, etc. The idea is for someone to pick up your portfolio and be impressed by you and your work. Two to three examples should be enough for most industries; however, it depends on the industry.

I emphasize tailored because this is ALWAYS better. I always shoot for the stars because at least I will land on the moon; however, even if you just put together a standard proposal package for a college fair, it will be impressive to recruiters. Remember, appearance is key. If possible, use good paper and bind the pages in a proposal cover that has a clear plastic front.

For a college fair, I would have up to five of these, being sure I have the best paper and cover for my top choices.

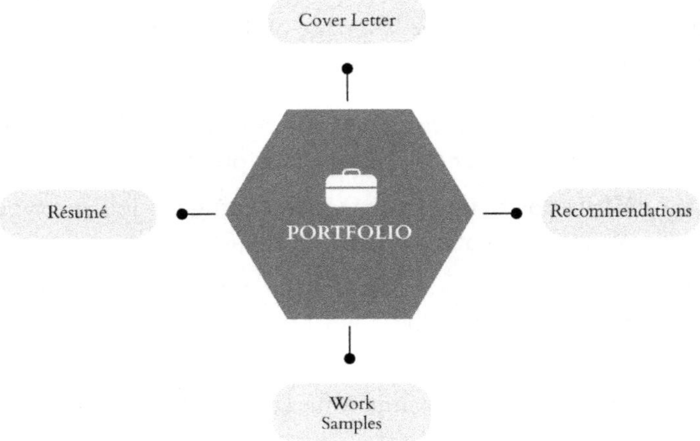

Exercise P4.5 – Developing a Working Portfolio

Using the information above, develop a working portfolio for your field.

Pay attention to the following:

- How you approach people will determine their reaction.
- To present yourself as the ideal candidate you must know what it is that people and organizations want.
- Do research to identify what they want and their language.
- Based upon your research, tailor what you say and what you present to their ideals. Speak their language.
- Practice this by developing talking points for every environment and interaction you have.
- When preparing for events that may lead to opportunities, craft an elevator conversation that introduces who you are, your goals, and lays the foundation for an engaging conversation.
- If you have practiced the above, interviews will be a piece of cake because you will have conducted your research, identified what their ideal candidate would be, developed answers to expected questions with practiced stories about yourself that uses their language, and engaged them with the confidence and comfort of a friend.
- All the above should be applied to anything you write, including cover letters, essay questions, and personal statements.
- If you are on a job hunt, a working portfolio that includes a tailored cover letter, résumé, recommendation letters, and work examples will put you in the highest echelon of candidates.

The Two Costs of The Academic Hustle

Everything you do costs time and money. Invest wisely.

Money Is Time

There is a popular adage that says, "time is money." Living in capitalistic society makes it easy to take this to heart. However, this is wrong.

Time is our most precious resource. Everyone has the same 24 hours in a day. It is what we do with our time that makes a person an engine technician or astronaut. Doctors, lawyers, congressmen, and engineers all have invested their time into becoming who they are. They have chosen to invest their time in medical school as opposed to law school, or politics as opposed to engineering. They chose career development as opposed to TV, games, or surfing the internet. Time is like money when invested in developing a career that produces valuable returns.

You can invest time to make money, but you cannot invest money to make time. Manufacturing companies have invested time into making products that we exchange for money. They invest the time in making a shoe and we give them money in exchange. Plumbers and counselors have invested time in their expertise and we exchange money for their services. *Money is created by people investing their time in creating products or services of value.* That is why money is time and not vice versa.

As you think about how much money you want to make, you must also think about how much time it will cost. Our 24 hours of time each day must be spread among eating, sleeping, working, leisure, family, friends, and many other things. To ensure that you develop in your career, it is critical to invest your time into things of value and manage the money you produce.

Invest Your Time

All great achievements require time
—Maya Angelou

When I conducted my research on high-achievers in school and in their careers, the top habit that participants said led to their success was time management. It was not surprising, at all.

In this section you will learn to:

- Select the best tools for you to manage your time.
- Develop your own personalized time management system.
- Organize your personal and professional life.

During my freshman year in college, I can count on one hand how many times I hung out with friends. I rarely went to the movies, out to party, or just chilled. That was purposeful. I needed to figure out this college stuff. I didn't have the slightest idea about how to write a research paper, study for tests, or anything that had to do with being a good student. I didn't know about extracurricular activities or the importance of creating good relationships. I knew that college was designed to help a person make more money in life, but I didn't know how. School needed to be paid for and I had no idea how to do it. But, I was determined to find out. I knew that there were 'A' students. I knew that people won scholarships. All I needed to do was figure it out and that's all you need to as well.

As with all things, the easiest way to figure out anything is to read or ask someone. Therefore, I spent all my time reading about how to read a book (I still have the book on my bookshelf as a reminder of how far I have come), how to study, how to apply for scholarships, how to become a student leader, and anything else I could get my hands on that would improve my chances of paying for school. I was a little too arrogant to ask for help back then. I took a lot more time to read and reread my books for class. I wrote and rewrote papers. I studied and studied some more. I was desperate, and I put in an astronomical amount of time to become better. As you can see, it paid off. That experience taught me one of the most valuable lessons in life: **You can be and do whatever you want if you put in the time to do what it takes.**

Everything in life is about how we invest our time. All our success and failures can be attributed to this. Lebron James has become one of the greatest players in the NBA because he has put in an astronomical amount of time studying and practicing the game. Doctors are doctors because they have allocated their time to the profession. Your best friends are your best friends because they have spent a lot of quality time with you or you've had a lot of great times with them. It is all about *time.*

Time is the one resource you can never get back. Yet, there are so many things that demand a certain amount of your time. If you do not manage your time, you do not have control of your life. If you do manage your time, then you are the master of your life.

Time management is a very simple matter, all it takes is a notepad, an agenda, and most importantly, a little time!

1. Notepad
   You need to have a notebook, a small notepad, or an app. This is for writing out all your tasks and organizing them.

2. Agenda
   Depending on how many things you have going on and how intense your schedule will be, you need to get a daily, weekly, and/or monthly agenda. This can be in the form of a notepad or an app.

3. A little time
   Ten minutes at the beginning or end of your day is all you need. At the end of the day, is the most useful because you

can review how well you performed throughout the day and get everything you need in place for the next day.

The whole point of time management is in doing three things: identifying what you need to do, setting a time to do it, and actually doing it.

Identifying What You Need to Do

None of this is rocket science. When identifying what you need to do, simply look at your life and list all the things you need to get done. Take this one step at a time. If you are using time management for school activities, then it is as simple as thinking about each class and extracurricular activity and listing out all your tasks. If you are applying this toward your life overall, then think through the things you must do using the following list:

1. **Roles –** Student, friend, son, organization president, etc.

2. **Goals –** I want to get a 4.0 GPA; I want to join the soccer team

3. **Projects –** Science fair, group project, scholarship search

4. **Requests –** From people or activities, assignments

5. **Expectations –** Based upon your roles and activities

6. **Ideas –** Random thoughts or wishes

Take out your notepad and *write* what you must do. It is extremely important that you write these things down. The whole point of this process is to get those things you need to do out of your head and on to paper so you can see what you must do. This is the first step.

Next, save yourself the stress of being overwhelmed by categorizing your tasks. For example, this could be a list for a specific class, activities you have to complete around the house, or a goal you have. If you have a big task to do like fix the roof or write a paper, then break them down using this model:

Goal: Complete Research Paper by Friday

Objectives:

- Complete literature review
- Complete methodology
- Complete introduction/statement of problem
- Complete conclusion
- Complete bibliography
- Review and proofread

Tasks

- Ask friend if they would proofread paper
- Ask professor for insight on where to find the best articles for literature review
- Pick up laptop from friend
- Identify ten articles for literature review
- Identify quotes from two books for literature review

You want to write tasks down in simple short steps so that you are clear on what you must do, how long it will take you to do it, and when you must do it. Once you have all your tasks out of your mind and on paper, then it is time to figure out when you are going to do them.

Exercise T1 – Preparing for Time Management

Purchase a notebook and agenda. I know you may have some version on your phone, but there is something powerful to physically writing it all down. Be thoughtful on what kind you purchase. You want to make sure you enjoy carrying it around. Start your notebook by listing out the roles in your life and detailing the goals, projects, requests, expectations, and ideas associated with each.

Making Time to Do It

Step two is the tricky part. You must review your tasks then decide which task is more important and when is the best time to do it.

First, pull out your calendar and block out the times you have already committed to the following:

- Sleeping
- Eating
- Hygiene and housework
- Traveling
- Work/classes/meetings
- Standard leisure activities (TV show, hanging with friends, etc.)
- Other commitments

As you begin to plan each month, week, and/or day, ask yourself:

"What is the most important thing I must do?"

Go through your lists and label the tasks with the following:

- A – Things you must do today, this week, or within the month
- B – Things you need to do soon, but can put off
- C – Things that can wait

Many times, you will have multiple As, Bs, and Cs. If so, number them according to which ones are more important. Then go through your task list and put them on your agenda.

Say for instance, it is Sunday, September 17th, 2017. I have a test in psychology class, a science fair project in two weeks, and I want to join the debate club. My list may look something like this:

Psychology class

- Study for test
- Organize class folder
- Do homework
- Ask teacher what I can do to get an A on this test

Science fair

- Ask mom to purchase science fair board
- Finish test results
- Ask my partner when we can meet to decorate the board

Debate club

- Research debate club online
- Talk to at least two debate club members

For Sunday, I would look through the list and come up with the following tasks for that day.

Sunday

- Study for psychology test – A1
- Ask mom to purchase science fair board – A2

- Research debate club – C

I'm telling you, this will reveal much to you. Doing a simple exercise like this every day will put you on the track to achieve major goals in your life. Always break big tasks down into smaller tasks. To do this, simply ask yourself:

"What is the immediate next step?"

If you must plan an event for an organization, you can break the task down into many smaller tasks:

- Secure location
- Set agenda
- Secure speakers
- Create marketing plan
- Develop flyer

To break one of these tasks down even further – secure speakers

- Develop list of potential speakers
- Confirm with board
- Call speaker #1
- Call speaker #2
- Send confirmations to speakers
- Get speaker biographies

I would have a goal and then develop the first list which is everything I have to do for that item. Usually, these are tasks that may take more than one sitting. Then as I think about each task, I would break it down even further into daily (one-action) tasks. Those daily tasks are what would go on my agenda.

When planning for the month, I have no more than ten goals. As I start to plan my week I would break those goals down to smaller tasks. For example, my month task list may look like this:

Priority	Week	Task	Notes
A1	1	Write research paper for English class	Possible topic?
A2	1	Study for finals	
B	2	Plan SGA event	
C	3	Join the Debate club	Talk to Latesha

When I get to my weekly planning I would pull from my task list (which includes my monthly list) and create the following:

Priority	Day	Task	Notes
A1	M	Do preliminary research to select a topic for research paper	Talk to Carmen
A2	Tu	Read ch.8	
A3	W	Create outline for paper	
B1	W	Create study guide for ch. 8	
B2	Th	Write initial draft	

Try your best to think about how much time it will take you to complete each task. Be realistic by reviewing your schedule and thinking about what you need to do.

If you want to learn more, then there are plenty of good books and articles on time management. However, practice makes perfect. The more you take the time to manage your time, the better you will get at it. You will start to figure out what works. What are too many tasks? What time of the day is best to do planning? What is the best notebook for me? **Continue to perfect YOUR system. It is THE most important thing you can do to change and direct your life. When you manage your time, you become the master of your life. You create the life that you want to live.**

Exercise T2 – Executing Time Management

Review Exercise T1. Select and prioritize the tasks that can be done this week. Using your agenda, assign the tasks to days and times during the week. Review and edit your tasks each day. At the end of the month, review this system and improve based upon your lifestyle.

Doing It

I had to include this section in here. We all have dreams and wishes. Things that we want to do but can't find the time or energy to do. There are a lot of articles out there about overcoming procrastination – the greatest demon of them all. Procrastination is a strong force that we must constantly battle with. She is one of my biggest enemies.

The simplest way to overcome procrastination is to just do it. I know that sounds so simple that it's aggravating, but nobody is going to make it happen for you, but you. When it comes time to do what you must do – DO IT. Continuing to do what you don't want to do repeatedly will build a muscle called mental fortitude. If you want to be a high-achiever in all the things you want to do, then you must develop powerful mental fortitude. Develop the ability to get things done. Embrace what you must do when you have to do it. I take that back, not what you have to do, but what you *should* do. It is a privilege to get to the next level and make your dreams happen. It takes discipline to develop mental fortitude but once you have it and keep exercising it, life will only get easier.

One of the ways you can practice discipline and develop mental fortitude is by having an agenda and doing what you said you were going to do when you said you would do it. Even if you only do it for 5 minutes, make yourself start and then do it. If you stop, put yourself in the position to DO IT again. There are plenty of "tricks and tips" you can find online. I have used almost all of them. But at the end of the day, it all boils down to just doing what you have to do.

Getting Organized for Classes, Extracurricular Activities, & Applying

As you begin to get involved in things, become a great student, and an all-around awesome person, you will become busy. If you are not organized, items and tasks will get lost in the everyday shuffle. To ensure that you don't lose anything major, you must become organized.

Making time management a daily habit should address most of these concerns. However, keeping all your materials for your activities together in a consistent place will go a long way. You should be able to go to one folder, bin, or area on your desk and find almost everything you need for a class, extracurricular activity, or a project. Below are a few ways to keep yourself organized for various activities:

- **Class** – As mentioned before, have a notebook with pockets for **each class**. Yes, I know that was the telltale sign of a geek, so if you're still sensitive to what everyone thinks of you, be smooth with it or something. One of the pockets should have all handouts and another should have all completed assignments. If you have more than one pocket, consider using them for class projects, group activities, and related information. On your computer, you should also have a folder for each class. All your assignments, resources, and references for each class should be in this folder. Try your best to create subfolders to keep similar or related items together. It's all about compartmentalizing. Problems arise when you run one aspect into another.

- **Extracurricular activities** – Having a separate notebook for extracurricular activities is a smart idea. Usually, one notebook should be enough for all your activities outside of class. However, something that requires a lot of attention, like being president of a large organization, may require a separate notebook. A file folder on your computer and phone is also a good idea.
- **Projects** – When working on a project or a major task, it is very important that you keep everything in one place. You should have a file folder and notebook that has everything related to the project.

Everything should have its place. The more organized you are, the more time you will save and the less stress you will have. Continue to think about how you can become more organized. It is not an innate talent; so, don't take it for granted. People pay serious money for assistants who merely set up and maintain these kinds of systems for them. You don't have the money for that kind of expense but remember that you are just as important. Being organized is a habit developed over time that will serve you well throughout life.

Exercise T3 – Organize Your information

Purchase simple folders with pockets and space for notetaking for each class, extracurricular activity, and project. When you check your agenda each day, make sure you bring the folders associated with the activities of the day.

In summary:

- If you master your time, you will master life. It is one of the most important habits to develop.
- All you need to master time management is a notebook, agenda, and a little time.
- Time management involves identifying what you need to do, making time to do it, and doing it.
- Review your life daily to identify what you need to do and write it down. Break those tasks down into steps. Prioritize each one and assign a time to do it.
- Create an organization system for your classes and extracurricular activities. Each class should have a separate folder.

Manage Your Money

Money is not the only answer, but it makes a difference.
—Barack Obama

This chapter's objectives are designed to:

- Help you figure out the costs of your education.
- Find ways to pay for your career development.
- Show you how to manage your personal finances.

As stated before, money is exchanged for value. To make money in our society, we must provide services or produce products of value. In the education and career development arena, we must become valuable to receive money. That is the point of *The Academic Hustle*. We are trying to:

1. Pay for our education.

2. Make money to sustain ourselves and have awesome experiences while in school.

3. Set ourselves up for a career that will provide the income we want for our lives.

This is the last section in the book because you must develop value BEFORE you can earn money. The more value you place on your education, experiences, relationships, and presentations, the more money you will earn.

The funny thing about money is that you must have money to make money. Money is both the means and the result. Money pays for your education and experiences. As you build these, develop good relationships, and tailor your presentation, you put yourself in the position to earn money. However, money won't just jump into your lap once you become valuable. You must identify and take advantage of opportunities to express your value.

Once you do that, people will exchange money for the value you can create for them.

Another thing about money is that it comes and goes. It is not about how much money you make, but what you do with it (or in many circles, how much you can keep). As you earn money, you will spend money. Managing money is a balancing act between expenses and income. The balance between these two things is one of the most important factors to living a healthy life. You don't want to be sitting on milk crates for chairs and wiping your behind with newspaper while stacking away a fortune. At the same time, you don't want to be the fool driving a top of the line Benz, draped in designer clothes and getting migraines over how you're going to pay the rent. Peace of mind with your finances relieves stress. Sure, we all could use more, but to make moves in a reasonable, smart fashion is truly living the good life. That is where a good understanding of personal finance comes into play.

Do not sleep on this section. If you manage your money well, you will live well. At nineteen years old I was living in another state on my own with a thousand dollars coming in each month. I had a whip with a new lick and two twelves in the trunk (this is Miami talk for a car with a new paint job and really loud speakers). My roommate and I lived in three-bedroom house near campus. You *may* be able to imagine how much fun a nineteen-year-old with his own place, a car, and money can have when in an environment with thousands of people his own age and no parents around…I enjoyed life. You can too if you implement these lessons.

Understand the Costs

Everything costs. Knowing those costs is the first step to gaining control of your personal finances. As you work to develop our career, you will come across opportunities. Each of those opportunities costs. If you are going to school, there are application fees, tuition, books, etc. If it's joining an organization, then there may be membership fees, costs associated with attending events, or even travel costs. If you are working, there are costs associated with travel, food, and clothing. Having a firm grasp on these costs will give you a clearer idea on what you must do.

Ask yourself "What are the costs?"

When I was in school, I was acutely aware of all the costs of school:

- Tuition
- Room
- Board
- Books
- Supplies
- Student fees
- Travel
- Entertainment
- Application fee
- Lab fee
- Parking

I had them written down and calculated for every year I was in school. Once I knew the costs, all I had to do was figure out how I was going to cover them.

In whatever you get into, you must identify the cost. You will have to pay them one way or another. Just because you did not realize that there was a refund check fee or that traveling to and from an opportunity takes a lot of gas, does not mean you won't have to pay it. Too many people get into financial trouble because they didn't account for the costs. Look at what you must do and identify all the costs associated with it. Be very clear on the costs of every opportunity before you engage in them and know when they must be paid.

Exercise M1 – Identify the Cost of Education

Review the costs of your chosen educational path. Each educational institution should have a tuition and fees statement that would be available on the website, in the financial aid office, or student accounts office. Use this document to calculate the costs for each semester. Total the cost for the whole program.

Once the costs are identified, you must figure out how you are going to cover them.

How to Make Money

Once you understand what you want and why you want it, you will start to be amazed at how opportunities to make money will pop up in your life. The more you talk to others about what you want and why you want it, the more opportunities will pop up. When you go after what you want, do the research, start to look for opportunities, read, and act, you will consistently find opportunities come across your path.

Opportunities to make money are all around us. Almost everything you want to do has some type of training, class, book, organization, job, or program out there that will take you closer to your goal. All you must do is identify what you want and begin to figure out how to get there. As you start to take classes, get involved, and create relationships in your field, you will hear about countless opportunities to get to where you want. If you excel in what you do, then you will set yourself up to take advantage of the opportunities to get paid.

I have intentionally put this at the back of the book. If you have done or are doing what you need to do to become a competitive candidate, then you will run into quite a few opportunities to be awarded money for school. Paying for school is more of a matter of determination than finding opportunities. If you are determined to try every possible avenue available to you to find money for school, then you will find the money.

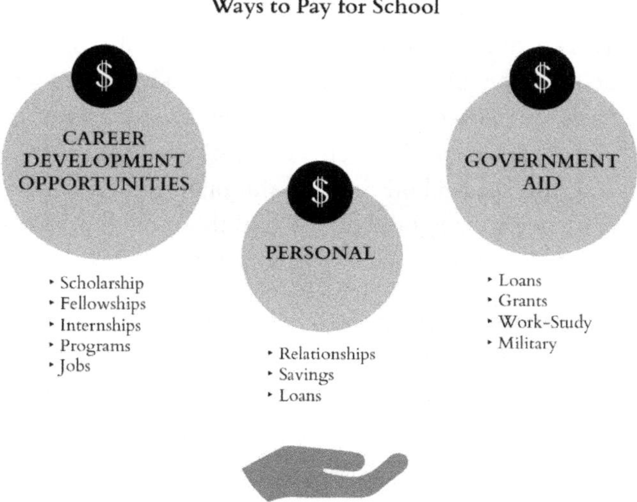

One of the first steps in securing funding for school is to explore any options provided by the government. In America, federal and state governments offer thousands of dollars in assistance to people furthering their education. As with almost all opportunities, you must apply. Once you complete the Free Application for Federal Student Aid (FASFA), schools will provide you with the following options:

1. **Loans –** Loans are debt. They will put you in a hole. Think of every $10,000 in loans as $75 a month you will have to pay for decades. Trust me. No matter how much you think you may need the money for other expenses, be frugal with loans. Use them only as necessary to cover the direct costs of school. Once you submit your FASFA, various types of loans options will be shared with you. Pay attention to the payback terms and the interest of each loan.

2. **Grants –** A grant is money given to your institution to cover costs. You do not have to pay this back. They are

usually automatically awarded based upon your situation. However, you should ask the financial aid office at the school you are applying to just to confirm if there are any that you may qualify for.

3. **Work-study –** Work-study is an opportunity to work on campus while attending school. Usually, it is a low stress job. This opportunity is usually awarded based upon your financial need. If you were not awarded this, ask your financial aid office about this opportunity. Some departments may be able to award this too you if available. They may also be called Teaching Assistantships.

The office of financial aid at the school will have all the information necessary for you to take advantage of these opportunities. Remember to *be kind*. The people in that office are aware of many ways to pay for school. Kindness can literally earn you thousands.

This book sets you up to take advantage of ways to pay for school that also serve to further your career development. These are:

1. **Scholarships –** Scholarships are money awarded to you to further your education. Schools, businesses, and non-profits, and governments (SBNGs) award them. Some are given directly to you and others are sent to your school. If your scholarships exceed your school expenses, you can get the excess refunded directly to you.

2. **Fellowships –** Fellowships are scholarships of distinction. When awarded a fellowship, you become a part of a society dedicated to developing in a certain area. They provide access to more opportunities, a powerful network, and training for what you want to do. Foundations are the main institutions that grant fellowships. However, some businesses, non-profits, and governments may award them as well.

3. **Programs –** This is a huge pool of opportunities that develop you in a certain area. They range from research programs, student exchange, to studying abroad. Departments within an institution usually put most programs together.

4. **Internships –** Internships are temporary jobs. Businesses, non-profits, and government entities provide them. Perusing a website or contacting their offices are usually good ways to identify them. You can also ask if they can create an internship for you.

5. **Jobs –** Jobs are the primary way people develop income. Many jobs pay for their employee's education. If you have a job, you should inquire about any opportunities to further your education.

There are four institutions that provide the above opportunities:

1. **Schools –** Schools usually give out the largest amount of scholarships. Those tuition, room, and board scholarships make up a huge chunk of your costs. When trying to pay for school, your main focus should be on getting the institution's scholarships. Next, look at the school's website for additional scholarships.

2. **Businesses** – Businesses are goldmines for opportunities. Look up businesses in your field and check their websites for scholarships, fellowships, internships, programs, and jobs (SFIPJ).

3. **Nonprofits** – There are plenty of organizations in each field that have opportunities you can take advantage of. Check their websites or visit them in person.

4. **Governments** – Federal, state, county, and city governments house a plethora of career development opportunities. Many of them are sponsored by grants. Be

sure to check out their websites and call, especially if you hear about a new grant they received.

There are literally thousands of schools, businesses, non-profits, and governments that have opportunities that you can take advantage of. You must sift through them to find the ones that you are most likely to get. The ones you are most likely to get are the ones you have the best connection to.

To get an idea of the career development opportunities in your field, you need to develop a list of keywords:

- **Know yourself –** Analyze yourself. Review your past experiences and future goals.
  - What organizations have you been a part of?
  - What extracurricular activities have you gotten involved with?
  - What areas are your awards in?
  - What are your goals, interests, passions, talents, skills, and strengths?
  - What classes did you perform well in?
  - What classes did you enjoy?
  - What do you like to do?
  - Where do you see yourself?
- **Know your field –** Get to know the field(s) that aligns with your background, interest areas, and career goals.
  - What are the SBNGs associated with your background and interest areas?
  - What is your *dream job*?
  - Who are the Who's Who in your field and what SBNGs have they been a part of?
  - What career development opportunities have they taken advantage of?

- What are the periodicals (magazines, journals, newspapers, etc.) in your field? Review them and list the SBNGs that are mentioned and are advertising in them.

Note the nouns and descriptive words discovered during the above analysis as *opportunity keywords* for your search. Combine these *opportunity keywords* with SFIPJs and SBNGs when conducting online searches for career development opportunities or asking people. For example, if your dream job is to become a neurosurgeon, you would enter the following in a search engine:

- "Top medical schools," "top corporations in the medical industry," "medical businesses in Florida," "medical associations," "medical foundations," "medical organizations," "health associations," "health organizations"

- "Top surgery schools," "top surgical instrument companies," "surgical centers in Florida," "surgical centers in Miami," "surgery associations," "surgery foundations," "surgical organizations"

- "Medical programs," "medical scholarships," "medical fellowships," "medical internships," "surgical jobs"

- "Biology programs," "biology scholarships," "biology fellowships," "biology internships"

Start your search as general as possible, then narrow it down to specializations. Begin by researching SBNGs in your field. You want to go directly to the awarding institutions to find out the details of each opportunity. If you come across databases that do not lead directly to the applications on the SBNG's website, copy the name of the opportunity and put it into a search engine until you find the actual application. Be wary of databases that do not lead to actual applications on SBNG's websites. Also, take caution with any contest scholarships. Usually their purpose is to get your information. Put most of your time into opportunities that require you to submit more than just an essay. If the opportunity only asks for your contact information and an essay or video, it may be a scam.

Below are some of the best places to find career development opportunities:

1. **Relationships –** The career development opportunities you will have the best chance of securing are going to be through your relationships.
    - The best place to start is with your *family* and *friends*. Find out the SBNGs they are connected to and what SFIPJs they have.
    - The next best place to identify SFIPJs is through the relationships you have built by *getting involved* and *taking classes*. If you have excelled in your work and developed pleasant relationships with the people involved, then the instructors, students, coordinators, and/or your bosses should be more than happy to share their resources. Get to know people, let them know your interests, and ask them about any SFIPJs they know about.
2. **Schools –** Your current and future school will be the greatest resources for identifying career development opportunities.
    - **Faculty –** Teachers write most of the recommendations to these opportunities. Many sit on the selection committee for SFIPJs and know quite a few students who secured them. Ask them.
    - **Staff –** Many schools have people whose job it is to know about SFIPJs. Financial aid staff, scholarship coordinators, career specialists, and guidance counselors are just a few. Also, don't forget the secretaries. A lot of resources pass through the department and many times they post them around the office.

- **Students –** There are students at your school and future school that are taking advantage of SFIPJs. Connect with them and learn how they are doing it.

3. **Your hometown or local community –** Approach local SBNGs in your city, your industry, or that align with your interest, values and what you like.

4. **Databases –** There are plenty of databases that have thousands of career development opportunities. Simply put "scholarships," "scholarship database," "summer research programs," "top internship sites" into a search engine and you will find quite a few. Also, you can go to your local library or bookstore to find books that have tons of scholarships.

Identifying the right opportunities to go after is a large part of the process for applying to SFIPJs. It takes work. But, not as much work as those who apply for everything, or those who waste their time going after sweepstake opportunities. The more targeted in your approach, the better. Remember Pillar #4. Every application you submit must be tailored! Therefore, you should be looking to apply to things you believe you can give the best presentation of yourself to.

Crash Course in Personal Finance

When the costs have been identified and you have income coming in, then you must make sure you allocate your income to take care of yourself in life. That is where a budget comes into play.

Managing your time and money for career development are the basis of your life in this society. When thinking through these two things, we must include all other aspects of our lives; the time and money you spend with family and friends will affect the time and money you spend on your career development. Therefore, your budget must include all these things.

A budget is simply a way to make sure you can do what you want. You allocate a certain amount of money to a specific category so that you have enough to take care of other categories. A budget should be developed and reevaluated at least monthly. Here are the basic things that should be included:

- **Shelter –** This includes all the costs associated with living somewhere: rent, mortgage, lights, water, gas, maintenance, moving fees, cable, internet, etc.
- **Food** – Everything you put in your mouth whether it is a snack picked up at a gas station, a dinner out with friends, or groceries. All of this should be accounted for.
- **Transportation** – All costs associated with however you get to and from wherever you must go need to be accounted for. If you have a car, that means gas, insurance, maintenance, parking, etc. If you are using public transportation, it will be as simple as the cost to ride.
- **Personal care –** Getting your hair cut, nails done, clothes dry cleaned, and many other things that you do to maintain your appearance, including health maintenance expenses, must be factored in.

These are your fixed expenses. They shouldn't vary much month to month. Below are some additional categories that need to be taken into consideration.

- **Personal enjoyment –** We all need a fun in our lives. Whatever that is for you, video games, going out to eat, partying, soccer, shopping, etc., make sure you budget your money for it.
- **Savings –** This is not an option. Saving money is critical. Rainy days happen. Emergencies happen. And there are things we want that we cannot pay for immediately. We need to save to cover these things.
- **Debt** – For those who have no debt, you are awesome. Try your best to stay away from it, especially credit card debt. Debt is like a hole that needs to be filled. All you are doing is throwing money down the hole to fill it, so

you don't have to worry about it anymore. Investment financing is the only debt you should take on. Investment financing is debt that will produce a return (i.e. bring in more money), which is basically your education, home, or a sound business plan.

- **Miscellaneous** – There will always be costs that are unaccounted for: gifts, tickets, late fees, unexpected food, shelter, or transportation costs, etc. As you begin to keep a budget, you will see a pattern and allocate how much money you need to take care of random expenses.

Everyone's budget will look different. We all lead unique lives and our budgets reflect that. For each of us, the above categories will be broken down in various ways. However, these are the standard categories you must account for each month. There is one more category, essential to anyone following *The Academic Hustle*.

Opportunity & Personal development – These are expenses associated with getting the right education, developing an impressive résumé, and building quality relationships. There will be membership fees, registration costs, transportation expenses, food bills, and a lot of other costs. If you budget for this, then you will know which opportunities you can and cannot go after.

Allocating your income across the above categories is the hardest part. How you allocate your income will vary from month to month. However, having standards is a good rule of thumb. The standard that I try to follow is:

- **Fixed expenses (60 percent) –** Depending on your income, this can be very hard to do. However, if you try to keep your fixed expenses under 60 percent your life will thank you. Living below your means is rewarding.
- **Entertainment (15 percent) –** If we make our money, we should enjoy our money. Not doing so causes stress. Do it too much, and it will also cause stress when bills are due and unexpected expenses arise.

- **Savings/Debt (15 percent) –** At least 10 percent of all your income should go toward long-term savings that is rarely touched. The rest of your money should pay off any debt and save for other big-ticket items.
- **Opportunities/Miscellaneous (10 percent) –** This pool of money should continue to build month after month. The only time you dig into this is if you have an opportunity you want to take advantage of or miscellaneous expenses. Eventually, this can become an emergency fund of at least six months of living. Once you get to that point then most of your money problems will disappear.

I have followed this system for years. While others complain about money problems, I have rarely had any worries while following this standard. When my scholarships didn't cover school expenses, I tapped into my opportunity or savings budget. When my car had major problems, I tapped into my miscellaneous budget. When I wanted to go on a trip or take advantage of an opportunity, I tapped into my entertainment or opportunities budget. I always had money. The key is keeping fixed expenses below 60percent and letting the rest of the money pile up. Being sure to spend your pile of money only when you must or want to take advantage of an opportunity to have fun or develop yourself.

There is so much more to learn about personal finance. However, following these basic ideas will set a VERY strong foundation. This section is one of the most important in the book. Please don't take it for granted.

Exercise M2 – Create a Budget

Use the following steps to develop a budget:

1. Write out your school costs and fixed expenses.
2. Calculate the total costs for your upcoming semester.
3. Detail your current and confirmed income from grants, loans, work, gifts, and scholarships.
4. Subtract your total income from your total costs.
5. If you have a negative number, you must immediately work on securing income opportunities.
6. If the results are positive, allocate the remaining money into savings/debt, entertainment, and opportunities/miscellaneous.
7. Divide your semester budget into monthly allocations.

Bank Accounts and Credit Cards

Bank accounts and credit cards are good tools to use in your personal finance strategy.

When selecting a bank account, try to secure a checking account that has branches and ATMs that are convenient to your school, home, and entertainment areas, no minimum balance requirement, does not cost you to operate, and will not let you overdraw your account and incur additional fees. Many students fall victim to banks that have ATMs on campus but are not convenient when off-campus. Also, the fees associated with some checking accounts can cost you much more than you would like. Be careful and selective of the banking institution you decide to join.

Credit cards are a double-edged sword. If managed well, you can lay the foundation for excellent credit that will save you thousands of dollars later in life and assist in major purchases. If not handled well, it will cost you thousands of dollars and hinder you from making major purchases later in life. Keep in mind the following when using credit cards:

- Secure only one credit card
- Find one with the lowest interest rate possible
- Never use more than 20 percent of the amount available
- Pay the balance each month
- If you cannot pay the balance each month, let no more than 10 percent of the available credit revolve to the next month

These tips may seem counterintuitive to having a credit card. However, the point of the credit card is not to be able to spend more money – it is about building your credit. Following these tips will ensure that you build an excellent credit score over time. I was able to buy my first house at 25 years old using this information.

Understand these points:

- Money is earned through the exchange of value.
- Managing money is all about balancing your income and expenses.
- Identifying the cost associated with life and what you want to do is the first step.
- Once you have a handle on how much things cost, then secure the income opportunities that will cover those costs.
- There are many career development opportunities that will pay you to attend school. These scholarships, fellowships, grants, work-study, jobs, programs, internships are available from schools, businesses, non-profits, and government institutions.
- Identify career development opportunities in your field and make the time to apply for them.
- How you allocated the money you receive is just as important as earning it. Create a budget and stick to it.

Developing Award-Winning Applications

Success is a journey, not a destination. The doing is often more important than the outcome.
—Arthur Ashe

Your application is a declaration of yourself as the ideal candidate for an opportunity. There are two parts to that declaration: being the ideal candidate and getting them to realize that you are. The clearer you are about the career development opportunities you want to take advantage of, the more strategic you can be in getting the education, experiences, and relationships that will transform you into the ideal candidate. This section summarizes the previous chapters by helping you establish how you can be strategic with the ***Four Pillars*** and become a competitive candidate for jobs and higher education, as well as the monetary benefits of scholarships and awards you can win along the way.

Let me let you in on some inside information: jobs, colleges, programs, and scholarships want you just as much as you want them, if not more. Businesses need you to increase their revenue. Colleges need your tuition and/or the recognition and donations you may bring in once you graduate. Programs want you, so they can fulfill their mission and grant requirements. Organizations that award scholarships want the attention you will bring them and bragging rights. That's why they are accepting you or awarding you money. They want you to be an awesome part of their team. They want a "poster child." Therein lies the secret to submitting a winning application: *be their poster child. Be the person that can fulfill their mission and vision.* Or…at least make your application sound like you would!

This is important because far too many of us suffer from (as I said earlier) the imposter syndrome, of thinking we're going this route, but we feel we are not deserving or competent enough to truly achieve what it is that we are pursuing. Far too many of us, therefore, are content with looking like we are about something, or forever talking about something we are about to do. You must accept that you are worthy of all that you pursue regarding *The Academic Hustle*, and that a setback here and there is not a total indictment of you not being cut out for the next level. It's just you are growing on your journey.

Your journey will include encountering institutions that are willing to give their money to you: the person they believe will fulfill their mission and vision. They are literally investing in you as a person. As with all investments, you need to strive to look like you will produce the highest returns with the least amount of risk. Great products sell themselves. That is why the major part of this book gives you insights and methodologies to *become* a competitive candidate. This section shows you how to market yourself as the best investment.

When you apply to something, whether it is a scholarship, program, college, or job, all of them are going to ask you four basic questions.

1. What do you know?
2. What have you done?
3. What do people say about you?
4. What do you say about yourself?

These questions are asked in a variety of ways, but they are the same thing. Your goal is to find out what are the answers that would make you the most competitive candidate.

What do you know?

Selection committees want to know what you know. What is your educational background? Depending on the opportunity, they may state a preference for a certain degree. They may ask for your transcript. They may want certain certifications. Whatever the case may be, they will be looking at the following in varying degrees:

1. The school you attended.
2. What type of degrees or certifications you received?
3. What was your major(s) or concentration?
4. What classes did you take?
5. How you performed overall (GPA and any honors)?
6. How you performed in certain classes related to them?

These things will have already been set in stone when you apply. That is why it is important to identify what your career goal is as early as possible. If you have identified your career pathway and what you are planning to apply to along the way, then you can do the research to find out how to develop the educational experiences that will make you the most competitive candidate.

Questions five and six will be covered by getting as many As as possible. It is very important to get As, especially in the classes that matter most to your next step. When doing research, you want to look at the top schools for your next step, what degrees or certifications are required, what should you major or concentrate in, and what specific classes will give you the education you need. For example, if you wanted to become a nuclear physicist, you will do your research and find out that Michigan State University, MIT, and the University of Washington are the top schools (question one) for nuclear physics. You will then target your efforts to getting into those schools and do more research to find out what it takes to get into those schools. You'll find out that you will need to get a PhD (question two) in physics with a concentration in nuclear physics (question three). Through your concentration, you will take the classes (question four) you need to specialize in nuclear physics. Finally, you will ensure that you get As in all your physics, math, and nuclear classes. If there are any awards you can get to make yourself look any more awesome as a nuclear physicist, you will make sure you go after them.

Remember, you must be strategic in how you answer each question. You must identify your next step, do your research to understand what the best answer to the questions above will be, and set yourself up to become that ideal candidate.

What have you done?

When selection committees ask this question, they are looking at your experience. Your experience includes any jobs you have done as well as the extracurricular activities you have participated in. Most selection committees will ask for your résumé, CV, a list of activities, any honors or awards you have, or ask you to describe your relevant experience. What they will be looking at is:

1. What experience do you have in the field?
2. How well have you performed in them?
3. What have you accomplished?
4. What are your involvements?

Most selection committees want to see a well-rounded person. Someone that is not only book smart but has also gained practical experience through various involvements. These committees want to know what you have done.

As you get involved, you will accumulate accomplishments, experiences, and accolades. You'll put ALL of those in the "master" résumé we discussed earlier. When applying for an opportunity your goals are to:

1. Identify what they want.
2. Select the experiences that speak to what they want.

3. Tailor the language used to describe those experiences to show them that you have what they want.

This tailored list of selected experiences will be what you present to them when they inquire as to what you have done. Being strategic and making sure what you do aligns with your career goals will help you develop an impressive list of activities to choose from.

I knew from my freshman year that I would be going to graduate school. At the time, I was shooting for a PhD because I wanted to become a professor. I did not know what area I wanted to get a PhD in, but I investigated what it took to become a competitive candidate for a PhD program. I knew the PhD process places a heavy emphasis on conducting research, doing presentations, and getting published. Therefore, I made sure I got involved in as many research programs as possible. I chose the programs that specifically trained students for academia; hence UNCF/Mellon Mays Fellowship and NIMH-COR. I got involved in research labs, conducted research, and presented at as many conferences as possible. I tried my hardest to get published in an academic journal but was unsuccessful. However, my paper for a conference was published online. Nonetheless, knowing what my next step was and doing things to make me a competitive candidate put me far ahead of my peers.

What do people say about you?

It is good to see that you have excelled in your education and have great experiences, but if no one can honestly say anything good about you, then your likelihood of being selected is slim. Almost all selection committees want to know what others think of you. Most people rarely take just one person's word about themselves or the product and services they offer. We like to check around and see what other people have to say. Hence, selection committees ask for recommendations and references. They want to have another person's stamp of approval before committing their own.

When answering this question, you want to make sure that the people and what they say about you align with the opportunity. Be strategic about who says what about you. How will the selection committee view the person referring you? How does the reference relate to the opportunity? What can they say that would make those offering the opportunity want you? How relevant would their perspective be? These are some of the questions you should ask when thinking about a recommender.

Also, share your *complete* application with your recommender and ask them to speak on the most important points of what the opportunity wants. If there is an experience or two that you have had with your recommender that you believe would be key to sharing with the selection committee, remind them of that experience and ask them to speak on it. You are the one that has done your research. You know the opportunity and what they want. Try to remove as much of the guesswork from your recommender/reference as possible. Make it easy for them to be a tailored part of your complete application.

What do you say about yourself?

Everything you apply for will ask you to talk about yourself and why you should be selected. For jobs, this usually takes place through the interview process. For colleges, scholarships, and programs, there is a heavy emphasis on short essays or writing samples. The main reason that they are asking you this is because they want to get an idea of your personality and your goals. Your answer to their questions should be based upon how you relate to them, which means you need to get a very good idea of who they are and what they are looking for.

Once you have a good idea of who they are, what they are looking for, and the language they use to describe themselves, throw it right back at them. What I mean by this is that you want to *tell stories of your experiences that relate to what they want using* ***their language and values.***

The language is a very key component. *Remember, if you want to be something, you must speak the language.* If you have done your research to find out what are the best answers to the questions above for a specific opportunity and you give them what they want, you will have put together an award-winning application. All applications have their own nuances, but the elements are the same. Figure out the elements and nuances for the specific opportunity you are going after and use these questions to guide you in compiling a tailored application.

The Complete Guide to Winning Everything

We have covered quite a few topics in this book. Now it is time to put it all together. Below are the steps to getting accepted into an educational program, winning scholarships, securing fellowships, taking advantage of internships, getting a job, and developing a prosperous career:

1. Become a competitive candidate – Read pages 55 - 217
    - Identify your what and why – Exercises F1.1-2
    - Invest your time (read pages 221-234) and money (read pages 235-251) into developing the following for your what
        - The best education – Exercises P1.1-4
        - An impressive résumé – Exercises P2.1-11
        - Powerful relationships – Exercises P3.1-5
2. Identify the opportunities – Exercise M2
3. Narrow your list based upon the deadline, requirements, your eligibility, and what is best for you – Read pages 227-231
4. Research the top opportunities – Read pages 189-193
5. Put together an award-winning application – Read pages 207-217
6. Submit your application
7. Follow up with an email confirming receipt, a call/email the following week, and check-in with them with a call/email periodically unless they advise otherwise
8. Manage the money you receive – Exercise M3

9. Record your accomplishments and what you do – Exercises P2.11

10. Be thankful – Read pages 13–15

There are no shortcuts to career development.

Read and complete the exercises.

Final Words

Once you have the game plan, all you have to do is HUSTLE.

We must *handle our business* to ensure we provide for our ourselves and our family. What we have done in the previous pages is apply the principals of *hustling* to the academic environment and your career development. It does not matter what happens in our lives - we must handle our business to be able to provide. *It is what it is*. EVERYONE has their challenges. If we were to honestly compare our challenges with others, we would most likely keep our own. To *hustle* means to *be strategic* about *handling your business* despite the circumstances. *We must do what we must do.*

I have given you the game plan. If you complete every exercise in this book, I guarantee you will earn money while developing you career. If you do not earn money while developing your career after completing these exercises, get your money back for this book by emailing info@theacademichustle.com.

Now with that reassurance, it is on you to *HUSTLE.*

About The Author

Recognized as Legacy Miami Magazine's 40 under 40, The *Miami Times*' New Generation of Dreamers, and Harvard Business School's Young American Leaders, Matthew A. Pigatt became the youngest elected official in South Florida in 2016 as Commissioner for the City of Opa-locka.

Commissioner Pigatt graduated magna cum laude from Morehouse College with a Bachelor of Arts in African American Studies and Psychology. As the first in his family to go away to college, Commissioner Pigatt earned over $100,000 while in school and participated in international research training programs in Paris, France and Dar es Salaam, Tanzania. He conducted national award-winning research at UC-Berkeley, Emory, and Morehouse on high-achieving individuals. After returning home he organized the Juvenile Justice Committee of People Acting for Community Together which assisted in the elimination of out-of-school suspension in Miami-Dade County Public Schools.

Currently, Commissioner Pigatt chairs the premier mentoring program for boys in South Florida, the 100 Black Men of South Florida Leadership Academy. He is the founder of the annual South Florida HBCU Picnic, founder of the Sankofa Cypher: A Black History, Culture, and Thought Group, and author of *The Academic Hustle: The Ultimate Game Plan for Scholarships, Fellowships, and Job Offers*. Through *The Academic Hustle*, Commissioner Pigatt has helped thousands of students secure millions in funding to attend school and develop their career.

The Academic Hustle: Online Course for Scholarships, Fellowships, Internships and more!
Access 30+ lessons detailing the scholarship application processes. Includes course guides, workbook, scholarship tracking tools, and videos

The Academic Hustle Curriculum for Instructors
The Academic Hustle Curriculum provides instructors of after-school programs, high school class and freshman orientation programs step-by-step lesson plans on career development.

Book
Matthew A. Pigatt as a speaker.

Become a Patreon.

FIND OUT MORE:

Visit
www.TheAcademicHustle.com

Email
info@theacademichustle.com

Social media
@matthewpigatt

#TheAcademicHustle

CPSIA information can be obtained
at www.ICGtesting.com
Printed in the USA
BVHW041754181219
567095BV00014B/101/P